Ancient Egyptians

AND THEIR

Neighbors

An
Activity
Guide

Marian Broida

CHICAGO
REVIEW
PRESS

Library of Congress Cataloging-in-Publication Data

Broida, Marian.

     Ancient Egyptians and their neighbors : an activity guide / Marian Broida.

     p.   cm.

     Includes bibliographical references and index.

     Summary: Uses activities and handicraft projects to reinforce information about the clothing, architecture, writing, work, food, and religion of the Egyptians, Mesopotamians, Nubians, and Hittites who lived in the Near East in ancient times.

     ISBN 1-55652-360-2

     1. Middle East—Civilization—To 30 B.C. Juvenile literature. 2. Egypt—Civilization—To 30 B.C. Juvenile literature. 3. Middle East—Civilization—30 B.C.—Study and teaching—Activity programs—Juvenile literature. 4. Egypt—Civilization—To 30 B.C.—Study and teaching—Activity programs—Juvenile literature. [1. Middle East—Civilization—30 B.C. 2. Egypt—Civilization—To 30 B.C. 3. Handicraft.] I. Title.

DS57.B74   1999

939'.4—dc21   99-22707

                                      CIP

Front cover images: (clockwise) Foundation Figurine of King Ur-Nammu, bronze, Nippur, Third Dynasty of Ur, ca. 2112–2095 B.C., courtesy of the Oriental Institute of the University of Chicago; Thebes, Tomb of Huy, no. 40, back wall of hall, left-hand portion. A Nubian princess in her ox-chariot. Reign of Tutankhamun, Dynasty XVIII, 1334–1335 B.C., Davies and Gardiner, *Ancient Egyptian Paintings*, plate LXXXI, courtesy of the Oriental Institute of the University of Chicago; and ceremonial vessel in the shape of a Bull Head, Tokat, 17th–16th centuries B.C., Museum of Anatolian Civilizations, Ankara, Turkey. **Back cover image:** Egyptian model boat, ca. 1900 B.C. Copyright The British Museum, London.

All photographs courtesy of Marian Broida unless otherwise noted.

Cover design: Joan Sommers Design
Interior design: Tamra Phelps
Interior illustration: Corasue Nicholas

The author and the publisher disclaim all liability for use of the information contained in this book.

© 1999 by Marian Broida
All rights reserved
First edition
Published by Chicago Review Press, Incorporated
814 North Franklin Street
Chicago, Illinois 60610
ISBN 1-55652-360-2
Printed in the United States of America
5 4 3 2 1

In memory of

Rabbi David Wolfe-Blank

and Arthur Broida:

brightness through pain

Contents

The Egyptians   1

The Mesopotamians   47

Foreword

Professors who study the ancient world sit day after day reading clay tablets, stone inscriptions, or scrolls of papyrus written thousands of years ago and gazing at objects made by craftspeople long dead. Why do we spend our time in this way? If asked, most of my colleagues would probably reply: "In order to learn the lessons that the peoples of the past can teach us today." Nonsense! Although we can and do profit from a knowledge of the great ideas, deeds, and mistakes of the past, we enter the world of Egypt or Nubia, of Hatti or Mesopotamia, because it's *fun*! To give a personal example, I became a Hittite scholar because at the age of eight I read a book by C. W. Ceram called *The Secret of the Hittites* and was never able to shake the fascination that this civilization exercised over me. My mother, my classmates, and more recently my wife have often commented on my diligence and dedication to my studies. But the truth is, this is not work, this is *fun*!

Marian Broida has uncovered this secret and in *Ancient Egyptians and Their Neighbors,* reveals it to—of all people—children! This seems to me entirely unfair, for children already know a great many ways to enjoy themselves. Ms. Broida might have left the study of the ancient Near East to me and other professors. But there you have it!

This clever and well-informed book responsibly presents numerous activities and projects that open a door to the life of several peoples of the ancient world—Egyptians, Mesopotamians, Nubians, and Hittites. All of the activities accurately reflect ancient practices and can be carried out with readily available materials. So do try these at home.

Do you want to dress and walk like an Egyptian? Eat like a Hittite? Build a house like a Nubian? Just follow the directions given here and you'll get the hang of it in no time. You might even decide to make a career of uncovering the past. But if you do, please don't tell our secret. Let others believe you study the past for the grand purpose of furthering human knowledge—not because it's fun!

—Gary Beckman
Professor of Hittite and Mesopotamian Studies
University of Michigan

Time Line

Scholars disagree about many dates, especially early ones. Wherever you see the symbol ~ (it means "about") before a date, this is a date disputed by scholars.

Time periods can go by different names as well. Egypt was a single unified kingdom, and most scholars agree on names for the major Egyptian time periods, like "Old Kingdom" and "New Kingdom." But Mesopotamia was a land of many city-states and governments that came and went, and some scholars like to list all of them. You may see "Ur III period" on some time lines, or "Isin-Larsa." Some scholars split Mesopotamia into two regions, giving separate time lines for Assyria and Babylonia; others combine them, as in this one.

Nubian time lines also differ. For example, during the Kerma Kingdom, other people lived in Nubia who weren't part of that kingdom, and some books give them separate names. No time line could give all the information about every period in history, or we'd never get beyond a single year! This time line reflects the way we discuss ancient cultures in this book. It's a good starting point for readers who are just getting to know the Egyptians, Mesopotamians, Nubians, and Hittites.

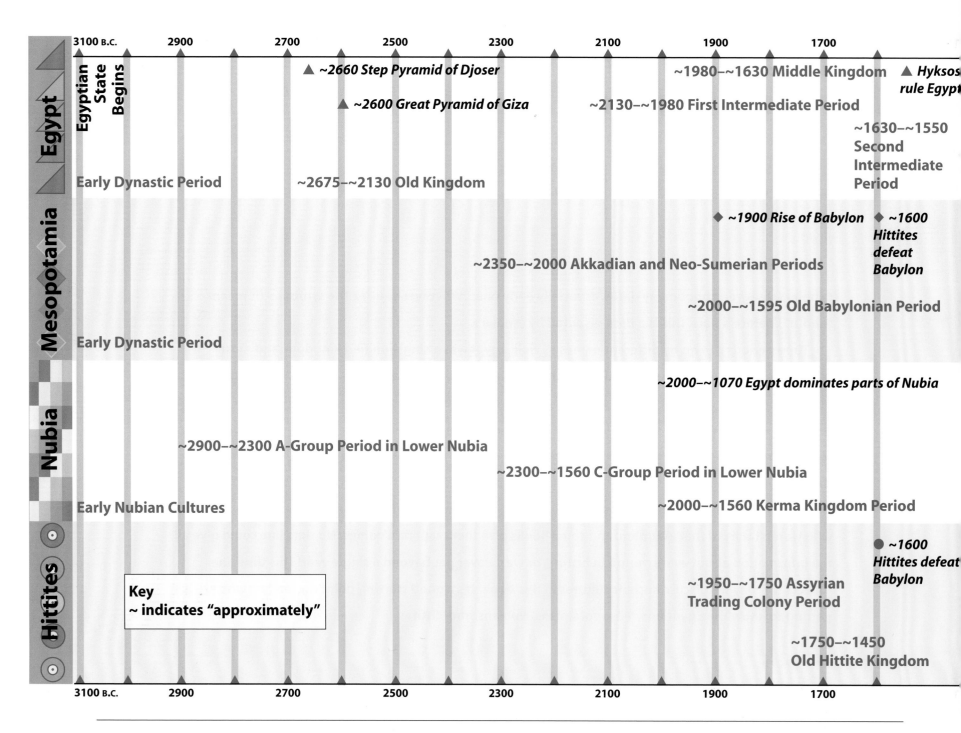

Egypt

~2660 Step Pyramid of Djoser

~2600 Great Pyramid of Giza

~1980–~1630 Middle Kingdom

~2130–~1980 First Intermediate Period

Hyksos rule Egypt

~1630–~1550 Second Intermediate Period

Egyptian State Begins

Early Dynastic Period

~2675–~2130 Old Kingdom

Mesopotamia

~1900 Rise of Babylon

~1600 Hittites defeat Babylon

~2350–~2000 Akkadian and Neo-Sumerian Periods

~2000–~1595 Old Babylonian Period

Early Dynastic Period

Nubia

~2000–~1070 Egypt dominates parts of Nubia

~2900–~2300 A-Group Period in Lower Nubia

~2300–~1560 C-Group Period in Lower Nubia

Early Nubian Cultures

~2000–~1560 Kerma Kingdom Period

Hittites

~1600 Hittites defeat Babylon

~1950–~1750 Assyrian Trading Colony Period

Key
~ indicates "approximately"

~1750–~1450 Old Hittite Kingdom

3100 B.C. | 2900 | 2700 | 2500 | 2300 | 2100 | 1900 | 1700

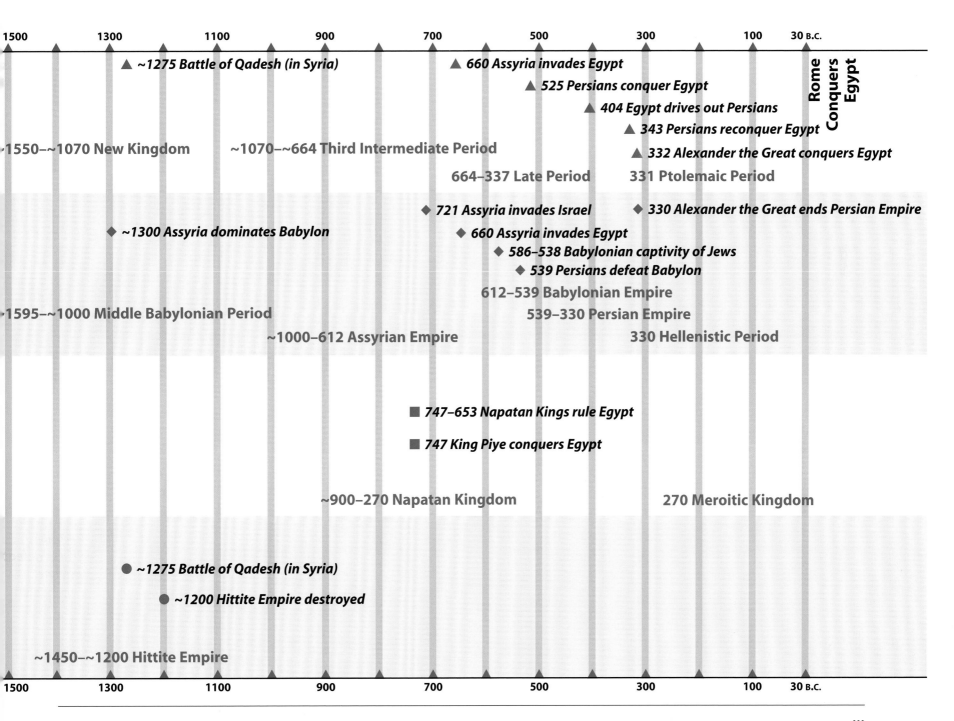

| 1500 | 1300 | 1100 | 900 | 700 | 500 | 300 | 100 | 30 B.C. |

▲ ~1275 Battle of Qadesh (in Syria) ▲ 660 Assyria invades Egypt

▲ 525 Persians conquer Egypt

▲ 404 Egypt drives out Persians

▲ 343 Persians reconquer Egypt

~1550–~1070 New Kingdom ~1070–~664 Third Intermediate Period ▲ 332 Alexander the Great conquers Egypt

664–337 Late Period 331 Ptolemaic Period

◆ 721 Assyria invades Israel ◆ 330 Alexander the Great ends Persian Empire

◆ ~1300 Assyria dominates Babylon ◆ 660 Assyria invades Egypt

◆ 586–538 Babylonian captivity of Jews

◆ 539 Persians defeat Babylon

612–539 Babylonian Empire

~1595–~1000 Middle Babylonian Period 539–330 Persian Empire

~1000–612 Assyrian Empire 330 Hellenistic Period

■ 747–653 Napatan Kings rule Egypt

■ 747 King Piye conquers Egypt

~900–270 Napatan Kingdom 270 Meroitic Kingdom

● ~1275 Battle of Qadesh (in Syria)

● ~1200 Hittite Empire destroyed

~1450–~1200 Hittite Empire

| 1500 | 1300 | 1100 | 900 | 700 | 500 | 300 | 100 | 30 B.C. |

Rome Conquers Egypt

Introduction

How did the ancient Egyptians live? Have you ever wondered? In this book you'll learn about life among the Egyptians and their neighbors thousands of years ago. You'll learn to build a model Egyptian step pyramid; follow an ancient Mesopotamian recipe discovered on a clay tablet; dress like a Nubian king or queen, complete with robe, royal shawl, earrings, and headdress; build a model of the oldest known machine for drawing water; create a Hittite pendant to wear; and much more.

This book will show you what life was like for Egyptians and their neighbors—people from other cultures who lived nearby. The Mesopotamians (meh-so-po-TAY-me-ans), Nubians, Hittites, Syrians, Libyans, and the people of Ebla, Elam, Susa, and Mari all lived in nearby lands at some point during the time of the ancient Egyptians. This book is about the ancient Egyptians and three of their neighbors, the Mesopotamians, Nubians, and Hittites.

The ancient Egyptian civilization lasted a remarkably long time—more than 3,000 years. During this time, cultures arose, prospered, and died out in neighboring lands and new cultures arose to replace them. For example, at different times, different cultures resided in the land we now call Israel. At some point in Egypt's past, the Canaanites (ka-NA-nites), the Hebrews, the Phoenicians (foe-NEE-shuns), the Philistines (FILL-i-stines), and others called parts of the land of Israel home.

The Mesopotamians lived in western Asia between the famous Tigris (TIE-griss) and Euphrates (you-FRAY-teez) rivers, in a country now called Iraq (i-RACK). The Mesopotamians included the Sumerians, Babylonians (bah-bih-LOE-nee-ans), Assyrians (a-SEE-ree-ans), and countless less well-known groups. Mesopotamia was powerfully influential. Its customs affect us even today. You practice Mesopotamian math whenever you tell time. Ever wonder why we have 60 minutes in an hour? It's because the Mesopotamians counted in 60s. They were also the first people to invent writing. This book will teach you how to make a model *ziggurat* (ZIG-goo-rat), a towering staircase for the gods like those the Mesopotamians built. The Bible story of the Tower of Babel was probably about a Mesopotamian ziggurat.

The Nubians were people who lived south of Egypt in Africa. They traded extensively with Egypt, sending gold, spices, and ostrich eggs in ships traveling north on the Nile. They built pyramids modeled on the Egyptians', and in later years invented their own alphabet. Their language—or languages—remain a mystery: only a few words of one language are understood today. Several Egyptian pharaohs were Nubians. Nubia, though far less powerful than Egypt, succeeded in ruling Egypt for 70 years.

Ancient Egyptians and Their Neighbors will teach you about the first Nubian king to rule Egypt, a man named Piye (pi-YAY), who loved horses and built the first pyramid in Nubia. You will learn to cook a dish with millet, a grain grown in Nubia, and make a model Nubian house from clay. You also will read about the fierce lion-god Apedemak, who was worshipped by the Nubians in later years.

The Hittites lived north of Egypt in the land we now call Turkey or Anatolia. Once one of the most powerful cultures in the region, they were forgotten for thousands of years until archaeologists began to uncover their ruins, and scholars discovered that the mysterious Hittite language was actually a relative of ours. You already know one word in Hittite. What comes from the sky in the form of rain? What flows in rivers in Anatolia and the United States? The Hittites called it "watar."

The Hittite kingdom lasted about 500 years. Fierce fighters, the Hittites conquered vast territories. You can read about their religion here—they claimed to have a thousand gods—and pretend you are a servant lost in their Great Temple. And you can copy an ancient sentence in actual Hittite writing.

▲　▲　▲

There are several reasons why Egypt is so much more famous than these other cultures. First, Egypt's dry desert air preserved things well. Colors stayed brilliant—reds, blues, and greens leap from the walls of tomb paintings to our eyes. Loaves of bread, linen dresses, even baskets of real figs have survived intact in the still air of the tombs. During the same centuries, many Hittite and Mesopotamian objects rotted away. The things that survived are those that couldn't rot—bronze statues, clay tablets, and silver harps. Second, mummies let us see how ancient Egyptians really looked. Scholars unwrapped the mummy of Ramses II, perhaps the most powerful pharaoh of Egypt, and learned he had a high-bridged nose and infected teeth. In contrast, most of the Egyptians' neighbors buried or burned their corpses, leaving only bones or dust for archaeologists to uncover. Third, the sheer number of objects found in Egypt is staggering. The tomb of an important lady held 77 linen sheets. Countless rings, bracelets, and necklaces of gold and

Telling Time

In this book, dates are expressed using the abbreviation B.C. to indicate years before the year 1 in the Roman calendar and A.D. for those years that follow the year 1. Some people express these date as B.C.E. and C.E.

Time is counted backward before the year 1. The bigger the number B.C., the longer ago something happened. About 3100 B.C. the first Egyptian king began his rule. That was more than 5,000 years ago. About 1200 B.C. the Hittite empire collapsed. That was only about 3,200 years ago. The number 3100 is bigger than 1200, so the Egyptian king ruled first.

Here's a trick to quickly tell how many years ago an event occurred. We are now near the year 2000. You can add 2,000 to any date B.C. and know how long ago something happened. In 30 B.C., the Romans defeated the great Queen Cleopatra. If the story is true, she allowed a poisonous snake to bite her, dying to escape from Roman control. Add 2,000 to 30 (from 30 B.C.) and you know that Cleopatra died about 2,030 years ago.

beautiful stones have been found. Glorious treasures did survive from the other three cultures, but far less. Much of it was probably melted down or stolen over the millennia.

People in the ancient Near East (as the region is called) maintained some customs that were harsh and cruel. All of these cultures kept slaves, often foreigners who had been captured in war. In the Mesopotamian city of Ur and the Nubian city of Kerma, dozens—sometimes hundreds—of the king's loyal subjects chose or were chosen to be buried with him when he died. In Ur, the subjects took poison first. In Kerma, they were probably buried alive.

▲   ▲   ▲

This book begins with the first Egyptian pharaoh, 5,000 years ago, and ends with the defeat of Queen Cleopatra by the Romans, 30 years before the year 1 B.C. It covers about three millennia—three thousand years.

How many people have lived and died since Cleopatra was captured, or the Hittites worshipped their thousand gods, or King Piye of Nubia first sat on Egypt's throne? Just imagine all those people, century after century, living their lives. More than 50 centuries—5,000 years—have passed since the earliest people in this book made their clothes, grew their food, raised their children, and told their stories. How amazing it is that we know anything at all about how they lived! Yet we know quite a lot—as you will see.

Trade Map of the Ancient Near East

Historians have discovered actual trade routes that ancient people used as well as some of the goods they traded. Trade is one way these ancient civilizations interacted. Try to follow the trade routes on the map and learn the distance between famous and not-so-famous cities and countries. (Note: Unlike modern maps, this map does not show borders of the countries. Borders changed many times over 3,000 years.)

1. It is 3100 B.C., the time that our book begins. You are bringing a cargo of blue stones from Mesopotamia to Egypt to be made into jewelry. Begin in the Mesopotamian city, Uruk. Travel by donkey to a town on the coast of Syria, called Tabara el-Akrad today. Here you board a ship and cross the Mediterranean Sea to the mouth of the Nile River. Battling wild hippopotami, you sail to the city of Memphis, where you unload your cargo.

2. Leap forward in time to 1850 B.C. You are traveling by donkey from the town of Ashur in northern Mesopotamia. You and hundreds of other traders are carrying loads of tin and fine woolen clothing. Travel north to the Assyrian city of Nineveh, then west to Carchemish (KAR-keh-mesh) in Syria. From here go northwest to the town of Kanesh in the land of Hatti, home of the Hittites. There you trade your goods for pieces of silver. You don't get coins—money hasn't been invented yet.

3. Come forward in time to 1650 B.C. You are bringing a load of olive oil and wine from southern Egypt to Nubia. Board your boat in the city of Thebes. Sail south on the Nile River past the town of Aswan to a group of rapids and waterfalls called the "First Cataract." To cross the cataract, the sailors must take down the sail. From the shore, they drag the boat around the rapids with strong ropes. Once past the rapids, the boat sets sail again. Twice more sailors must tow the boat across dangerous rapids and waterfalls, at the Second and Third Cataracts. Finally you arrive at the city of Kerma. You meet the Nubian king in his fine tall audience hall. There you trade your goods for gold, ivory, and ostrich feathers.

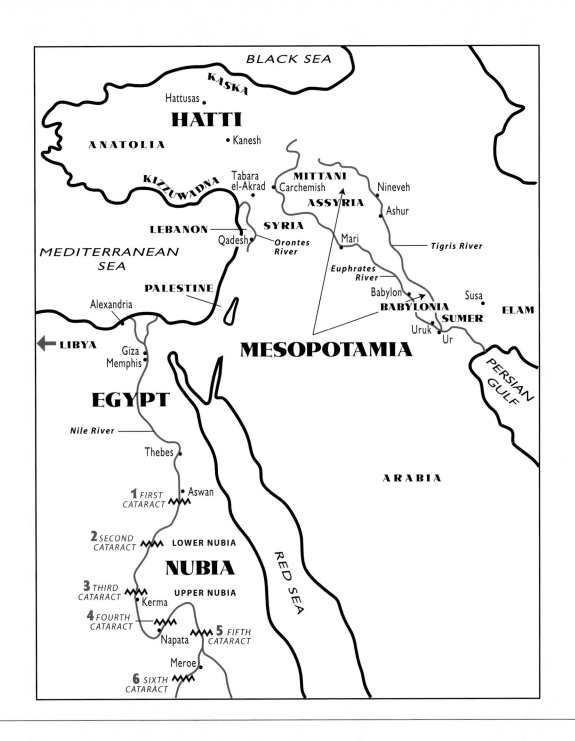

The Egyptians

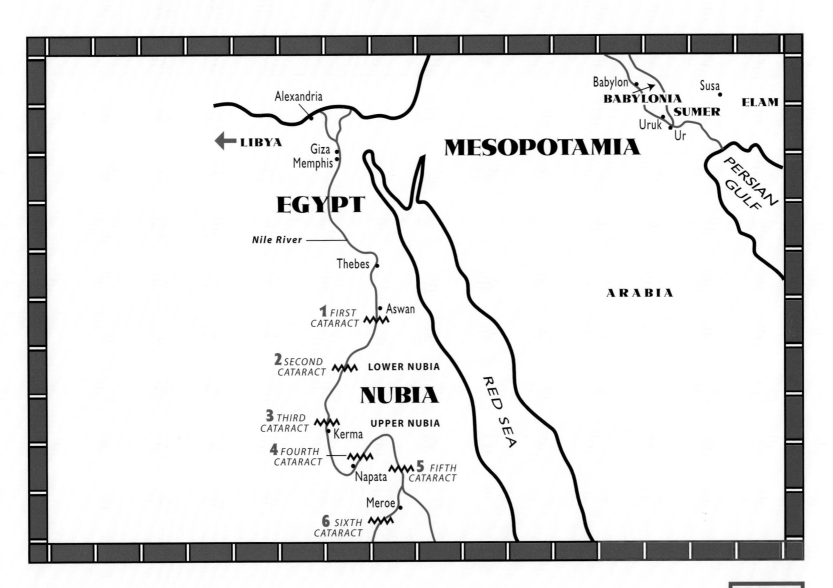

Babylon
Susa
BABYLONIA
SUMER
ELAM
Uruk
Ur
PERSIAN GULF

Alexandria

← LIBYA
Giza
Memphis

MESOPOTAMIA

EGYPT

Nile River —

Thebes

ARABIA

1 FIRST CATARACT 〰 • Aswan

2 SECOND CATARACT 〰 LOWER NUBIA

NUBIA

RED SEA

3 THIRD CATARACT 〰 • Kerma

UPPER NUBIA

4 FOURTH CATARACT 〰

5 FIFTH CATARACT 〰
• Napata

• Meroe

6 SIXTH CATARACT 〰

1

Egyptian History and Geography

The Nile River cuts through a valley in northeast Africa. Seen from the sky, the river is surrounded by a narrow band of blazing green on both sides. Beyond the green is dry desert. Stark red cliffs rise on either side of the valley.

The ancient Egyptians called their land *Kemet*, which meant "black land"—the rich black earth watered yearly when the Nile flooded. Crops grew only where the floodwaters moistened the land. Farmers learned to irrigate, so they could grow two or three crops a year before the flood waters retreated completely. Crops could not be grown in the desert, called the "red land." There was very little rain. Over most of Egypt the sun blazed down day after day, and only in the evenings did the air grow cool.

Ancient Egyptians believed that people could return to life after death, just as plants grew back each year with the Nile's flood. They believed that bodies, if preserved and reunited with their spirits, could enter afterlife (the life people led after leaving this world). They buried their dead with the supplies they would need for eternal life. They soaked pharaohs' bodies in a mineral called *natron* to preserve them as mummies. They buried the pharaohs in pyramids or rock-cut tombs meant to last forever.

The Egyptians spent much time preparing for the afterlife. They loved this life and they believed something quite like it would continue after they died. Tomb paintings show vivid pictures of people feasting and playing, as well as working hard in fields, workshops, and homes. Both rich and poor Egyptians played board games and enjoyed singing and dancing. They owed their lives and their pleasures to the gifts of the Nile—food, water, and transportation.

Nature made the Nile a wonderful means of travel. This huge river is the largest in the world running from south to north. While the current rushes one way, the wind blows the other. Nature helped ancient Egyptian travelers go in either direction. Boats could float with the current down the river to the north, and sail up the river to the south.

It was fairly easy to get from one end of Egypt to the other, but it was hard to get into Egypt from other countries. The desert, the sea, and fierce river rapids isolated Egypt from cultures on all sides. Its geography protected Egypt from most invaders. It also kept other cultures from greatly changing the Egyptian way of life.

Over the 3,000 years covered in this book, Egyptian culture changed in many ways—but not nearly as much as our own has changed in a shorter period of time. An Egyptian from 2800 B.C. would still recognize many ways of living in 300 B.C. Do you think a Native American or European from 500 B.C.—long before the beginning of the English language, many religions, electricity, or computers—would recognize anything in the modern United States?

Our book begins in 3100 B.C., the start of the first Egyptian *dynasty* (DIE-nus-tee), or family of kings. (Some scholars give that date as 3000 B.C., or even 2675 B.C.) Ancient Egyptians believed their civilization began when Upper Egypt united with Lower Egypt under a king named Menes (MEN-aze).

Egyptian history is usually sorted into periods of time called *kingdoms*. There were three kingdoms in ancient Egypt: old, middle, and new. The Old Kingdom began around 2675 B.C. In between the kingdoms were periods of conflict called *intermediate periods*. Sometimes during the intermediate periods more than one king claimed to be pharaoh. In two of the intermediate periods, foreigners ruled Egypt. People called Hyksos (HEEK-sose) ruled Egypt during one of them, and Nubians ruled Egypt during part of another.

After the New Kingdom came the Third Intermediate Period, followed by a Late Period. The Late Period ended in 332 B.C. when Alexander the Great conquered Egypt.

After Alexander's death, his general Ptolemy (TALL-uh-mee) and Ptolemy's descendents ruled, during a time called the Ptolemaic (tall-uh-MAY-ik) Period. The Ptolemies formed the last dynasty in Egypt. In 30 B.C. the Romans defeated the Ptolemaic queen Cleopatra, beginning Roman rule of Egypt. Cleopatra's death marks the endpoint of this book.

Egyptian Architecture

J utting into the sky, the pyramids look as if they will endure forever. The Egyptians meant the pyramids to inspire awe, both among the pharaoh's subjects and among foreign visitors. The builders strove to make the pyramids grand and glorious because they were meant for gods. The Egyptians believed their kings were gods. They wanted the tombs, like the gods, to last for eternity.

In fact these pyramids, especially the early ones, have held up remarkably well. The Great Pyramid of Giza was called one of the Seven Wonders of the World by an ancient Greek traveler Herodotus (her-ODD-o-tus) because it was one of the biggest man-made structures of the time. (The other six wonders were the Temple of Artemis at Ephesus, the Mausoleum at Halicarnassus, the Statue of Zeus at Olympia, the Colossus of Rhodes, the Hanging Garden of Babylon, and the Pharos at Alexandria.) Many of the pyramid's outer blocks were removed to build the modern city of Cairo. Even without its smooth limestone exterior, the pyramid still inspires awe.

The earliest Egyptian pharaohs were buried in mud-brick tombs called *mastabas* (ma-STA-bas), until a brilliant man named Imhotep (im-HO-tep) designed the first pyramid for King Djoser (JOE-sir), around 2660 B.C. Imhotep was the king's architect, as well as an astronomer, priest, physician, and scribe. He was called the eyes, ears, and hands of the pharaoh and was appointed the king's *vizier* (prime minister). He was such an amazing man that thousands of years later Imhotep was worshipped as a minor god. This first pyramid was later called the Step Pyramid because it looked like a staircase. In fact, the Egyptians believed the king would climb the steps to heaven when he died.

This pyramid is remarkable for many reasons. It was the first time people in Egypt used stone for building. Before then they used mud brick. Also, the architect kept changing his mind while building it. First Imhotep built a large mastaba. But that seemed too small, so he added two more levels. Even that was too small, so he enlarged the base and added more levels. In the end he built a pyramid that had six levels.

Imhotep did other things that were new and strange. He built many buildings surrounding the pyramid, including a temple for the king's statue and a temple where the king's body would be prepared for burial. But some buildings were fake. The outer walls were carefully carved and decorated, but inside the buildings were filled with rubble.

Imhotep built a huge stone wall surrounding the pyramid and all these buildings. He made what appeared to be 14 entrances to the stone wall, but only one was the real entrance. The other 13 were fake. We don't know why Imhotep built so many fake entrances. Maybe it was to fool grave robbers. But more likely it was for magical or religious purposes. He built the entire building complex to look like the pharaoh's palace and surrounding buildings. The Egyptians may have thought that the real palace buildings would go with the king into the next world if they built models of them near his tomb.

Simple Step Pyramid

Y ou can make a model step pyramid out of sugar cubes. Be careful of the ants!

Materials

- ▲ Newspapers
- ▲ 1-pound box (95 or more) sugar cubes (The cubes must be shaped like squares, not bricks.)
- ▲ Heavy paper plate
- ▲ Pencil
- ▲ Glue
- ▲ Small paintbrush

Directions

Spread out newspapers on your work surface. Arrange 36 sugar cubes in the middle of the plate. Make a square of six rows of six cubes each. Carefully trace around the outside of the square with the pencil. Remove the sugar cubes from the plate. Drizzle some glue within the outline, being careful not to get too close to the edges. With your paintbrush, spread the glue inside this box. Starting at one corner, replace the sugar cubes in the glue-filled square. Drizzle and brush more glue across the top of the sugar cubes, covering the inner 16 cubes completely. Arrange 25 more cubes on top of your square (five rows of five). They should cover the part you glued. Make another square of glue on top of this layer. Arrange four rows of four cubes on top of this second layer. Repeat this process for squares made of nine cubes and then four cubes. Finish with a single cube on top. To make a temple, place four cubes (two rows of two) next to one side of the pyramid base. Trace around them with a pencil, then glue them in place.

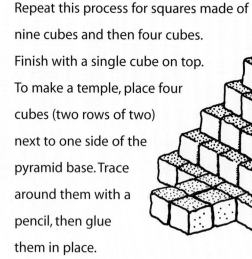

Houses for Everyday Life

The Egyptian sun beats down almost ceaselessly. Ancient Egyptians built their homes to avoid the heat. They used bricks made of mud, which helped keep the inside of the homes cool. They often made the main room taller than the others, with tiny windows high up in the wall. The heat rose during the day. The small windows, called *clerestory* (CLEER-story) windows today, let the hot air escape.

Most Egyptians built their houses with a flat roof, which they used as an extra room, with a ladder or staircase rising to it from ground level. People cooked and slept on the roof.

The ancient Egyptians loved gardens. Wealthy Egyptians would put a garden next to their homes. A rectangular pool formed the center of the garden. Colorful fish swam in the pool. White and blue lotus flowers floated on top alongside water lilies. Palm or fig trees bordered the pool, giving cool shade. In the heat of the day, the family would rest beneath the trees or on a porch beside the pool. The porch attached to the main house or to a separate small building. Painted columns, often shaped like trees or plants, supported the porch roof. The family could sit on the porch and enjoy the view of the water and plant life.

An Egyptian named Meket-Re had this model garden put into his tomb. Wooden fig trees surround a copper pool that can hold real water. During the Middle Kingdom, Egyptians often put funerary models into their tombs of things they wanted to have in the afterlife. *Meket-Re's Estate, residence A. Courtesy of the Metropolitan Museum of Art, New York. All rights reserved*

Egyptian Model Garden

This model porch and garden is adapted from an ancient wooden model (see page 9) discovered in a Middle Kingdom tomb. An Egyptian named Meket-Re sat with his family in a garden like this one.

Materials

▲ *Facial tissue box, 9¹/₄ by 4³/₄ inches*

▲ *Scissors*

▲ *Green and brown paint*

▲ *Paintbrushes*

▲ *Jar of water*

▲ *4 white 3- by 5-inch index cards*

▲ *Colored markers or other paint colors*

▲ *5 green (or white) 3- by 5-inch index cards*

▲ *Scotch tape*

▲ *Pencil*

▲ *Small piece silver or aluminum foil (about 2 by 4 inches)*

▲ *Colored paper*

▲ *Glue (optional)*

Directions

1. Cut off the top of the box, leaving a one- to two-inch lip covering one end. This is the porch roof. Pull out any plastic liner.

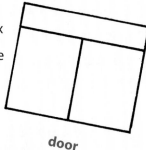

2. Paint the floor of the box green.

3. Make a door by cutting a white index card into a rectangle smaller than the width of one end of the box. Decorate it with markers and tape it to the short side of the box under the roof.

door

4. Make three pillars to support the roof, using a white index card. (Save the green ones for trees.) To make a pillar, first decorate

pillar

the plain side of the index card with wide colored stripes, using paint or markers. Paint the stripes horizontally across the short side. Then roll it into a skinny tube the long way and tape it closed. Make four small cuts ($\frac{1}{2}$ inch or less) around one end of the tube about $\frac{1}{2}$ inch apart. Fold out the four cut sections.

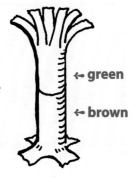

← green

← brown

5. Trim the other end so the pillar is about $\frac{1}{2}$ inch taller than the porch roof. Now make four small cuts in the other end and fold out the four small cut sections. When the floor is dry, place the pillar under the roof. Spread out the cut sections and tape them to the floor and ceiling. Make two or three pillars this way.

← $\frac{1}{2}$ inch cut

← tape

← tape

6. With the remaining index cards, make palm trees. First draw a line across the middle of the index card from one long side to the other (the short way). Paint the top part green (unless it's a green card), and the bottom part brown. When it dries, turn the card over and color the back of the green part green, too, so the top half of the card is completely green.

7. Roll the card into a tube the long way, with the brown and green parts showing, and tape it closed. Now make one- to two-inch-long cuts about $\frac{1}{4}$ inch apart all the way around the top. Fold down the cut sections to form palm leaves.

8. Make four cuts about $\frac{1}{2}$ inch long in the bottom of the trunk. Fold out the four bottom sections. In a little while you will tape these to the floor to hold up the tree.

9. Trim the silver foil and tape it to the bottom of the box in the middle.

10. Tape the bottoms of the trees symmetrically around the edge of the pond. The Egyptians liked symmetry, so both sides of the pond should be the same.

11. Cut out small ornamental fish, lotuses, and lily pads from colored paper and glue or tape them to the pond.

Now imagine you are sitting on your porch, enjoying a cool breeze off the pond as your palm trees sway.

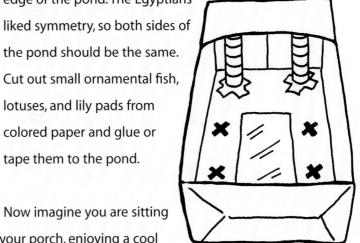

Trees go at ✖ marks with one more tree at the end farthest from the porch.

Egyptian Clothing

Egyptians wore clothes woven of linen made from flax plants. The weave could be coarse, for ordinary people, or so fine you could see through it, for the rich to wear on important occasions.

During most of Egypt's history, women did the weaving on flat looms set up on the ground. During the New Kingdom (~1550–~1070 B.C.), some men began weaving on upright wooden looms. Clothing was usually left white, bleached with chemicals or the hot Egyptian sun.

Two articles of clothing were popular, a plain *kilt* (skirt) for men and a long sleeveless dress for women. Both could

This family group shows a man named Meresankh with his two daughters around 2325 B.C. The younger daughter is named Hathor-wer, and the older one is Lymeret. Notice the girls' sleeveless dresses and the father's kilt. All three are shown wearing wigs. *Courtesy of Jürgen Liepe, Berlin*

be pleated. During the Old and Middle Kingdoms, Egyptian art shows men wearing kilts and women wearing long sleeveless dresses. During the New Kingdom, tomb paintings show more elaborate, looser clothing. Women and men are shown wearing clothes with sleeves and many pleats. Even so, pictures still show men wearing kilts and women wearing sleeveless dresses, sometimes with a shawl.

Children often wore nothing except jewelry and *amulets* (charms to protect them from evil).

Sometimes guests drank too much at Egyptian feasts and threw up. The Egyptians weren't shy about drawing pictures of them! Notice the cone of scented fat on top of the ladies' heads and the flowers they are holding. Perhaps the fragrances of the flower and the perfumed fat helped the lady recover. *Courtesy of Sir J. Gardner Wilkinson,* A Popular Account of the Ancient Egyptians, *Library of Congress*

Girl's Long Dress

Try making this long dress from a couple of pillowcases. You'll need help measuring. Then walk like an Egyptian!

inside-out pillowcase

Materials

▲ *2 old matching white pillowcases (or any solid color)*

▲ *Pencil*

▲ *Ruler or tape measure*

▲ *Scissors*

▲ *Safety pins or adhesive tape*

Directions

shoulder straps drawn

line drawn from armpit to armpit

Turn one pillowcase inside out. Take off any bulky sweaters and lie down on top of the pillowcase with the very base of your neck at the closed narrow end. Have a friend trace around your upper body with the pencil. Stop just below the arms. Get up, and draw a straight line from armpit to armpit on the pillowcase. Draw two wide shoulder straps on the pillowcase from the edge of your neck, extending to the armpit line. (Be careful to start right next to the neck.) Straps should be about two inches wide at the top, getting wider as they go down. Cut out around the straps (but not across the tops).

Try on the dress inside out. It may be too wide. Use safety pins to take in the sides. Leave enough room so you can get it off and on.

To make the dress longer, take it off, still inside out. Slit the end of the second pillowcase and turn it inside out too. Slide the cut end of the second pillowcase over the bottom of the first one, just past the hem. Pin them together and try the dress on. If it's too long, mark the length you'd like. (Egyptian paintings show women wearing ankle-length dresses.) Make a small cut at this desired length and then tear the cloth the rest of the way.

Turn the dress right side out and wear it with an Egyptian necklace or bracelet (see pages 18–20).

pins →

second pillowcase

second pillowcase
over the first

Shorten if necessary.

Boy's Short Kilt

Use an old pillowcase to make a kilt like the ones worn by Egyptian men and boys. You will need someone to help you measure.

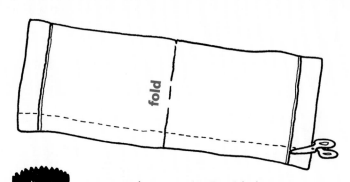

Materials

▲ *Old white pillowcase (or any solid color if white's not available)*

▲ *Scissors*

▲ *Straight pin or pen for marking*

▲ *Safety pin (optional)*

Directions

Cut along the two sides of the pillowcase, leaving the end uncut. Open the cloth into a long strip and wrap it

around your waist. Decide how long you want it. (Egyptians usually wore kilts above the knee.) Have a friend mark the length you want with a pin or pen.

Lay down the cloth. Cut the cloth at your mark. Then tear the rest of the way. Save the strip for a belt.

Wrap the pillowcase around you again. If you like, use a safety pin to secure it around your waist. Tie on the belt, leaving the ends in front. (You can tuck them in.) Wear your kilt with an Egyptian bracelet or necklace or (see pages 18–20).

16

Hair and Makeup

Ancient Egyptians wore their hair naturally or they wore wigs. Many people shaved their heads or cut their hair very short. Wealthy ladies and gentlemen sometimes wore elaborate wigs on fancy occasions. Children had shaved heads or very short hair except for a single lock of hair on the side called a *sidelock*. Cutting off the sidelock was a step toward becoming an adult.

Egyptians had some unique grooming traditions. Sometimes they wore a cone of scented fat on top of their wigs. In the hot air the fat melted, sending trickles of sweet-smelling grease down their wigs and bodies. Egyptians used scented oils and fats to keep their skin moist. Egyptian men and women also wore eye paint to help protect their vision from the sun's glare.

Egyptian Jewelry

Everyone in Egypt—rich or poor, infants or old people—wore jewelry. If they could afford it they wore gold set with gemstones: garnets, turquoises, a blue stone called *lapis lazuli* (LAP-us LAZ-oo-lie), or red carnelian. Egyptians favored heavy necklaces and collars made of beads. They also wore bracelets, armbands, anklets, earrings, and *pectorals* (PECK-tore-ulls), which were large inlaid pendants hung from bead necklaces.

Easy Egyptian Bracelet

Wear this bracelet on your wrist or upper arm. Combine it with the necklace, kilt, or dress for a real Egyptian effect.

Materials

- ▲ Newspapers
- ▲ Toilet paper roll
- ▲ Scissors
- ▲ Acrylic paints

- ▲ Paintbrushes
- ▲ Jar of water
- ▲ Fine-tipped black marker
- ▲ Stapler or tape

Directions

Spread the newspapers to work on. Slit the toilet paper roll open with a straight cut. Cut it in half the short way. Paint the outside of both halves the same way. You might paint them completely yellow to make them look like solid gold, or you might decorate them with blue and green stripes, going either direction. Once the paint is dry, you can outline your stripes with black marker or draw Egyptian designs on the solid gold.

Staple or tape the end of one band to the end of the other. Staples should point out. **staple**

Leave one end open so you can get the band on and off. Wear the bracelet on your wrist or upper arm.

Double-Stranded Necklace

You can make colorful beads, then string them into a necklace like one worn by Egyptian men and women.

Adult help recommended with the wire and the oven.

Materials

▲ Oven

▲ Waxed paper

▲ Ruler

▲ 2 squares polymer clay, such as Sculpey or Fimo, in different colors

▲ Table knife or similar clay tool

▲ Round toothpick

▲ 2 pieces wire (use the straight part of a coat hanger)

▲ Large oven-proof bowl

▲ 4 to 5 feet heavy nylon thread

▲ Scissors

▲ Glue, such as GS Hypo-Tube Cement, Super NEW Glue, or Elmer's Glue

▲ 50 to 80 medium-sized round beads

▲ Necklace clasp (available in craft and bead stores)

Directions

Preheat the oven according to directions on the clay. Lay out a piece of waxed paper on a table to work on. Use a knife to cut a square about $\frac{1}{2}$ inch thick out of one block of clay. With the toothpick, pierce a hole from one side to the other near the top. (To keep from deforming the square, poke the toothpick through the clay until you see it form a bump on the other side. Remove the toothpick. Then, coming from the other direction, poke the toothpick through the bump.) Add more clay if the bead is too thin and breaks when you poke through it! Now pierce another hole from side to side near the bottom. Make 12 square

Cut squares from clay.

bump → toothpick

beads of the same color. (You'll only need 10 beads, but make a few extra in case some break while baking.)

Now make another kind of bead from a different color. Cut narrow rectangles about ½ inch thick. (They should be just as thick from front to back as the squares.) Trim the sides so the top is narrower than the bottom, forming a triangle with a flat top. Make 12 of these. Pierce these beads only at the top. Pierce from side to side, just like the square beads.

String the beads on the wires so they are not touching. Lay the wires across the top of the bowl. Place in the oven. Set the timer for the time recommended on the clay (usually 10–20 minutes.) When finished baking, allow the beads to cool completely before stringing. Remember to turn off the oven.

triangle bead with flat top

While the clay beads bake and cool, cut the nylon thread in half. Tie the two pieces together at one end. Place one drop of glue on the waxed paper. Dip the knot into the glue. Then carefully dip the two untied ends of thread in the glue. Coat about one inch of the end of each thread. (This will stiffen the threads for easier beading.) Set the coated ends down on the waxed paper apart from each other and the knot, and let them dry.

beads strung on wire for baking

Begin stringing the beads to make a necklace. You can create your own pattern or match the one here for an ancient Egyptian look. Tie one part of the clasp on each end of the necklace. Trim off any extra thread and then hook the necklace around your neck.

Egyptian Writing

Writing was once a special skill that only a few people knew. In ancient Egypt, reading and writing were done by people called *scribes*. Scribes wrote official documents for the government or the temples. They wrote letters from one person to another. They also wrote down stories. Special scribes kept busy making copies of important writings. Ordinary people had to hire a scribe to read or write for them.

For important writings, scribes wrote on *papyrus* (pa-PIE-russ), made of the stems of grasslike plants that were pounded together in sheets. They wrote with pens made from the stems of other plants called rushes. They chewed the ends of the rushes to create writing tips. They used red ink, made from red ocher, and black ink, made from soot taken from cooking pots.

Ancient Egyptians didn't use the English alphabet. Scribes (especially priests) wrote in Egyptian *hieroglyphs* (HI-ro-glifs), a kind of picture writing. The pictures stood for things and for sounds as well. Scribes wrote or carved hieroglyphic symbols on temple walls, monuments, and very important documents.

At the same time, scribes also wrote in a kind of cursive called *hieratic* (hi-RA-tik). Hieratic looked a little bit like hieroglyphic writing but was faster and easier to write. Most writing was in hieratic, which is harder for us to read.

In the Middle Kingdom (1980–1630 B.C.) some boys entered a school for scribes around age 10. They learned to write by copying documents into hieratic on old pieces of pottery or wooden boards. (Papyrus was too expensive to use while learning.) Then they became apprenticed to a scribe, usually their father. Girls didn't become scribes, but princesses were taught to read.

In the late period, many people learned to read an even simpler kind of cursive writing called *demotic*. It looked nothing like hieroglyphic writing and was very different from hieratic. It was used more and more for nonreligious writing.

The Story of the Shipwrecked Sailor

Here's an example of a story written by a scribe.

An Egyptian sailor washed up on an island after a storm destroyed his ship. For three days he was completely alone. He was so lonely, he felt his own heart keeping him company.

Then he stretched his legs, looked around, and discovered there were many good things to eat on the island. He stuffed himself on figs, cucumbers, fish, and other delicious food.

Suddenly he heard a sound like thunder and felt the ground tremble. He covered his face in fear. When he uncovered his face, he found a gigantic snake before him—but what a snake! This snake was coated with gold. He had eyebrows of the blue stone called lapis lazuli, and a beard that was almost three feet long.

The snake asked the sailor questions, then picked him up in his mouth and carried him to another part of the island, where he set him down unhurt.

The snake told the man that in four months he would be rescued and taken back to Egypt. The man was so grateful he promised to send back shiploads of gifts. But the snake laughed. The snake said he didn't need the man's gifts because he already had fabulous amounts of wealth: precious incense, perfumes, and spices. He also said the island wouldn't be found again.

Sure enough, in four months' time a ship arrived from Egypt and took the man home. The snake gave the man many gifts to take with him: greyhounds, baboons, spices, and perfumes. The sailor arrived safely and gave his gifts to the king. In gratitude, the king made him his attendant. The sailor never saw the island again.

Hieroglyphic Writing

Hieroglyphs were a beautiful form of Egyptian writing. Every sign was a picture. Hieroglyphic symbols were often written from right to left, backward from how we read English, but sometimes symbols were written in columns and were read from top to bottom. Symbols were also written from left to right. Sometimes scribes wrote both ways in the same piece of writing, going from right to left on one line and left to right on the next.

Each hieroglyphic picture stood for a word and for the sound of that word spoken aloud. Imagine if we wrote the word "bee" in English by drawing a bee. If we wanted to write the word "be," we could use the same picture. The Egyptians did something like this.

Groups of pictures could also stand for a single word. The sign for "scribe" was a picture of a pen case, a palette with red and black ink, and a bag of water. These were the scribe's tools.

We can put together a sort of alphabet from 24 of the Egyptian signs. Most of these signs stand for a single consonant. This alphabet is missing all the vowels. Egyptians could understand writing even without them. English is harder to read this way than Egyptian, because of the way we spell. Bt prbbly y cn rd Nglsh ths wy f y wrk hrd.

The alphabet is also missing some English consonants, probably because the Egyptians didn't need them. Their language didn't have the sounds V and L. Instead, they used signs for some sounds that we don't use in English. One sign stood for a K sound made deep in the back of the throat. One stood for an extra-harsh H. Two more stood for sounds, sometimes spelled CH, which are common in other languages, such as Hebrew, Arabic, German, or Scottish.

Some clues help when you are reading hieroglyphs. The Egyptians surrounded royal names with a picture of curled rope, which we call a *cartouche* (car-TOOSH). When people saw pictures inside the rope, they knew those signs stood for the pharaoh's name. The Egyptians also used special signs to tell the reader what kind of word they meant. For example, after writing the name of a tree, they might put a sign that meant tree.

Egyptian Hieroglyphic Alphabet

These signs stand for consonants like those in our alphabet. If you are writing from right to left, draw them facing the other direction.

Sign	*Sounds like*	*Picture of*
	b as in boy	foot
	d as in dog	hand
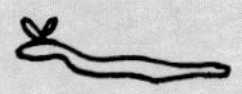	f as in fish	horned viper
	g as in game	jar stand
	h as in have	hut (top view)
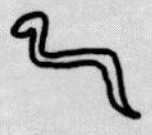	j as in just	snake
	k as in kite	basket
	m as in mouse	owl
	n as in noise	water
	p as in pig	stool
	q as in queen	hill
	r as in rat	mountain
	s as in sit	folded cloth
	t as in toe	loaf of bread
	w as in wish	quail chick
	y as in you	flowering reeds
	z as in zoo	door bolt
	ch as in child	rope tether
	sh as in should	pool

These signs stand for sounds unlike those in English.

Sign	*Sounds like*	*Picture of*
	extra-harsh h	twisted flax
	ch in German "ach"	uncertain
	ch in German "ich"	pig's belly
	swallowing deep in throat while talking	forearm
	stopping your voice instead of making a sound, like saying Sa'urday	vulture

Hieroglyphic Secret Note

You can use some Egyptian signs to write a secret note in hieroglyphs.

Materials

▲ *Hieroglyphic alphabet (see page 25)*
▲ *Paper*
▲ *Pen or pencil*

Remember to read from right to left. This illustration translates as Hw R Y. Add vowels and you get, "How are you?"

Directions

On page 25 is an Egyptian hieroglyphic alphabet. It's a little different from some Egyptian alphabets you may see, which include vowels. (So-called vowels in Egyptian are really consonants such as "y" and "w.") Try using this one to write a short note to a friend in English. Write from right to left, left to right, or top to bottom. Sign it with your name in hieroglyphs. Surround your name with a picture of a coiled rope, to make a cartouche.

Hint   When choosing Egyptian signs, think about how the English word sounds, not just how it is spelled. The name *Christopher* really sounds like Kris-to-fer. If a letter you want doesn't exist, skip it or pick one that sounds a little like it. You can use the letter for "r" instead of "l."

cartouche

This translates as J, N, F, R, or Jennifer.

Egyptian Work

The pharaoh was the most powerful person in the land. The ancient Egyptians believed the pharaoh was a god and that everything in Egypt, including every person, belonged to the pharaoh. He was supposed to be guided by principles of balance and harmony.

The majority of ancient Egyptians were farmers or laborers—often both. During the season when the Nile's floodwaters were receding, nearly everyone helped plant and tend the crops. When the Nile was in full flood, farmers could work as laborers, since the farmland was under water.

Pharaohs often ordered building projects—not only their own tombs, but also statues and temples to glorify a god or celebrate a victory. Pharaohs' officials forced people to work on these projects. The officials paid the laborers in food and clothing, since the ancient Egyptians did not use money. The laborers hauled the heavy stones on sledges and put them into place. It was hot, exhausting work.

Not everyone worked as a farmer or laborer. Some poor people worked as servants in wealthy or middle-class households. Women servants often worked carrying water or grinding grain—hard daily work. They ground the grain in stone troughs. A lot of stone grit got into the bread, which is why most mummies have worn-down teeth!

Men servants did the laundry using *natron* (NAY-tron), the same mineral that is used for mummification. Natron occurs as a natural crystal in a couple of places in Egypt. Laundrymen first carried the dirty clothes to a nearby stream or canal. There they washed them in two pottery tubs filled with water. They soaked the clothes in cold water in one tub while they lit a fire under the second tub and mixed in natron crystals. When the water was warm, they put in the wet clothes. Then they beat the warm, wet clothing on a large stone, using a wooden stick or paddle. Finally the laundrymen rinsed the clothes in the river, wrung them out and spread them in the sun to dry and bleach.

▲　▲　▲

Other Egyptians worked as specialized craftsmen. Metal workers smelted copper from ore in ovens called kilns, or combined tin and copper to make the metal bronze. Craftsmen shaped the metal into needles, tweezers, hoes, and other household objects and tools. Stoneworkers and potters made jars, bowls, and pots. Carpenters fashioned chairs and beds with legs like animals' paws. Builders constructed houses. Weavers made cloth.

Middle-class men worked as priests, scribes, physicians, or government officials. The middle class was small in the Old Kingdom (~2675–~2130 B.C.), but many people entered it during Middle Kingdom days (~1980–~1630 B.C.).

Women labored just as hard as men. Women farmed, made baskets, and sold goods in the marketplace. Some worked as paid mourners at funerals, as priestesses, or as dancers or singers at parties. Women did most of the household work. They wove, cooked, made bread and beer, and minded children.

Ancient Egyptian Laundry

You can do laundry with homemade natron. It's easy to turn this activity into a science experiment. Take two dirty white socks. Wash one using natron and one in a modern washing machine with detergent. See which comes out cleaner!

You can do this activity outside or in. It's safe to pour the natron solution on the ground, but not into a body of water such as a lake or stream. Do not touch your eyes or mouth while doing this activity. Thoroughly wash all utensils afterward.

Adult help recommended with the washing solution.

Materials

- ▲ 2 buckets or laundry tubs
- ▲ Cold water (from hose or tap)
- ▲ 3 or 4 pieces dirty white clothing or rags
- ▲ Bowl
- ▲ $1/2$ cup washing soda (sodium carbonate)
- ▲ $1/4$ cup baking soda (sodium bicarbonate)
- ▲ $1/2$ teaspoon salt
- ▲ Large wooden spoon
- ▲ Warm water
- ▲ Drying rack or clothesline (optional)

Directions

Fill one tub or bucket with cold water and add clothes. Make natron by pouring the washing soda, baking soda, and salt in the bowl. Use the wooden spoon to mix. Put the warm water into the second tub or bucket. Add the natron mixture. Use the spoon to transfer the clothes to the second bucket. Swish them around for a while. (Note: Natron doesn't form suds.)

Dump the water from the cold water tub or bucket and turn it upside down. Take a garment from the natron bucket, squeeze it gently, and lay it across the upturned tub. Thwack it with the wooden spoon a number of times to drive the natron into the fabric. Repeat this process for the other garments. When you are finished, you can dump out the natron water and store your washed clothing in the second bucket. Rinse the clothing under running water. Wring it out. Spread it out on the ground or a drying rack, or hang it out to dry.

How clean does the clothing look and smell?

Sailors and Ships

Besides providing water for drinking and crops, the Nile provided the main means of travel in ancient Egypt. Boats loaded with goods for trade, stone for building, or mummies for burial traveled constantly up and down the Nile. Sailors raised the sails that caught the breeze going south. They plied the oars pulling the boats north with the current's help.

Sometimes sailors journeyed to other lands, like the sailor in the story on page 23. Pharaohs sent ships to the mysterious land of Punt to collect frankincense, myrrh, greyhounds, and other luxuries. Ships sailed to Lebanon for cedar logs to build more ships. Ships voyaged to Nubia for ivory, gold, perfumes, and ostrich feathers.

This model boat was buried in a tomb around 1900 B.C. The large paddle at one end is really a rudder for steering.
Copyright The British Museum, London

31

Egyptian Sailboat

You can make a model Egyptian sailboat like some of those traveling on the Nile during Egypt's Middle Kingdom.

Materials

▲ Paper towel roll

▲ Scissors

▲ Ruler

▲ Pen or pencil

▲ Stapler

▲ Scotch tape

▲ Newspapers

▲ Acrylic or poster paints

▲ Paintbrushes

▲ Jar of water

▲ 3-by-3-inch sterile gauze bandage

▲ 2 pipe cleaners

▲ Wooden chopstick

▲ Miniature figurines for sailors (optional)

Directions

Make a straight cut with the scissors down the paper towel roll from one end to the other. You will have a long rectangle of cardboard that wants to curl up. Lay the ruler along one of the long edges and make a dot three inches from

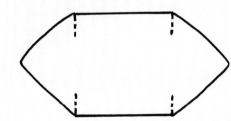

each end. Now do the same thing on the other long edge. (You will draw four dots, hereafter referred to as side dots.) Make a dot in the middle of each short edge (these are end dots). Draw a straight line connecting one of the side dots to the nearest end dot. Repeat with the opposite side dot. Do this for the two remaining side dots.

Cut the cardboard along each of the four lines you drew. Save the pieces you cut off. Now starting at one of the side dots, cut a one-inch slit toward the middle. Repeat this for the other side dots. Overlap the two edges of one of the slits as much as you can, and

end dot

3 inches

side dots

3 inches

end dot

staple. Repeat at the other three slits. You should now have a rough boat shape with a flat-bottomed midsection. Trim the edges near the staples to even out the shape. At each end of the boat, pinch the two sides together and staple at the very tip.

Make a holder for the mast by taking one of the cardboard scraps and trimming it into a triangle or rectangle about two inches at the base and three inches tall. On the two-inch side, cut four $1/2$-inch slits. Roll the cardboard into a narrow tube with the slits at the bottom, and tape closed. Fold back the parts you slit so the cut parts fan out on all sides. Tape them to the flat part in the middle of the boat.

Lay down newspapers. Paint the boat.

While the paint dries, make the mast and sail. Open the gauze bandage and unfold it so only two folds are left: one at the

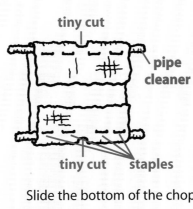

top and one at the bottom. Make a tiny cut in the middle of each crease. Lay a pipe cleaner inside each crease so only the ends stick out. Staple the pipe cleaners into the creases. (Be careful not to staple too close to the two cuts.) Slide the chopstick through the bottom cut, across the two pipe cleaners, and through the top cut so about $1/2$ inch of the chopstick sticks out of the top. Tape it into place against the gauze. Trim off the ends of the pipe cleaners where they stick out of the gauze.

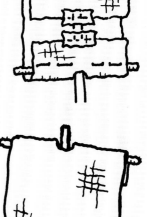

tiny cut

pipe cleaner

tiny cut   staples

Slide the bottom of the chopstick into the mast holder. If the mast holder is too tall and pushes up on the bottom of the sail, trim the top of the mast holder. If your boat tends to tip over, add cargo (small bundles or pebbles) or miniature people to keep it steady.

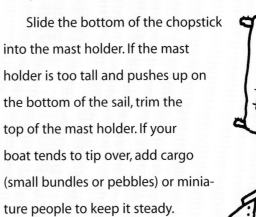

staple

staple

staple

Egyptian Food

Bread and beer were prominent parts of the Egyptian diet. The Egyptians considered these two foods the basics needed for life.

Egyptians made bread from two kinds of grain. One was called *emmer*, an ancient kind of wheat that was harder to hull than modern wheat. The other was barley. Most bread found in tombs was made with emmer wheat.

Bread was made to rise by tiny yeast organisms that floated in the air or lingered on the pot used for kneading the bread dough on the previous day. Some bakers may have added yeast created from brewing beer. Ancient bread was heavier than modern bread because it was made from emmer wheat and barley, which contain very little gluten, a substance that makes dough stretchy. The higher gluten content in modern wheat helps make modern bread lighter and fluffier.

The Egyptians also ate cooked cereals and cakes. They sweetened cakes with figs, dates, or honey. They made at least 14 different kinds of bread. Bread and cakes came in many different shapes. Triangles, circles, half-moons, cone shapes, and spirals like Swiss rolls appear in Egyptian paintings and have been found in tombs.

Tomb paintings show how bread was made. When making large amounts, the bakers poured dough into big pots and kneaded it with their feet!

The Egyptians also used emmer and barley to make beer. They used yeast to ferment the grain (turn it to alcohol), then flavored it with herbs, dates, or wood chips. They imported special beer from other countries in New Kingdom days—just as people do today.

The Diets of Rich and Poor Citizens

Poor people lived mostly on bread and beer. They combined these with homegrown vegetables such as lettuce, cucumbers, radishes, onions, and garlic, as well as peas, lentils, and beans. They caught fish from the Nile, which they sometimes ate smoked or salted.

Richer people ate more meat. Ox meat was popular. They also ate sheep and goats. In parts of Egypt, people—especially the less wealthy—ate pigs.

Wealthy people ate many kinds of fruit, including grapes, dates, melons, and some we don't see in the United States, such as doum palm fruit. They often drank fine wine instead of beer. For recreation, they hunted in the marshes, and then sometimes dined on their catch of hippopotamus or goose.

Pharaohs ate the best of all. King Unas, who ruled around 2600 B.C., could choose from milk; 3 kinds of beer; 5 kinds of wine; 14 kinds of bread; 10 kinds of cakes plus fruitcakes; 4 kinds of meat, goose, pigeon, and figs; 10 other types of fruit; 5 kinds of grain; 5 kinds of oil; and fresh greens. All of this might have been served at the same meal!

Because the Egyptians didn't use money, people often were paid in food. Official records of these salaries look more like grocery lists to modern eyes. High-ranking workers were paid in fancier food and in larger quantities—amounts unrelated to the intensity of their labor. For example, every day the man appointed the king's messenger and standard-bearer was given "good bread, ox meat, wine, sweet oil, olive oil, fat, honey, figs, fish, and vegetables." Meanwhile, laborers carrying heavy loads received "bread, two bundles of vegetables, and a roast of meat."

Most Egyptians ate seated on the ground or on chairs next to small tables, one table for every person. They ate with their fingers. Before and after eating, they poured water over their hands.

Overnight Fig Cakes

Here's one kind of pastry that the Egyptians might have eaten. It's heavy, just as ancient bread tended to be. **Adult help recommended with the oven.**

3 loaves

Ingredients

- $1/2$ cup very warm water
- 1 tablespoon plus 2 teaspoons honey
- $1/3$ cup whole wheat flour
- 1 package active dry yeast
- $1/4$ teaspoon salt
- 1 cup barley flour (available in health food stores)
- 1 (more) cup whole wheat flour
- 5 dried figs, chopped into small pieces
- Oil for baking pan
- 3 teaspoons (more) honey

Utensils

- Mixing bowl
- Glass measuring cup
- Measuring spoons
- Large spoon or rubber spatula
- Dishcloth
- Timer or clock
- Cutting board or clean counter
- Baking sheet
- Paper towel
- Oven
- Potholder
- Spatula

Directions

Rinse the bowl and measuring cup in warm water to heat them up. Place the very warm water into the bowl. Stir in the honey and $1/3$ cup whole wheat flour and mix well. Sprinkle in the yeast and stir gently just for a moment. If your kitchen is cool, cover the bowl with a dishcloth soaked in hot water and wrung out. Set the timer for 10 minutes.

After the timer goes off, stir in the salt and barley flour and mix well. Add the rest of the whole wheat flour. Mix together with clean hands. Add the chopped figs. Mix well. Divide the dough into three equal parts. With each part, make a snake about 12–18 inches long on the cutting board or counter. Then coil each snake into a spiral. Let the dough sit uncovered for six to eight hours or overnight in a warm place.

Preheat the oven to 375°. Use the paper towel to spread oil lightly on the baking sheet. Put the rolls on the baking sheet. When the oven is hot, bake the rolls for 15 minutes or until they brown on top. Remove from the baking sheet using a potholder and spatula. Remember to turn off the oven. Serve warm. Drizzle each with 1 teaspoon honey before serving.

Egyptian Religion

Egyptians believed in many gods and goddesses, including Ra, Osiris (oh-SIRE-us), Isis, Horus, and Amun. The Egyptians told sacred stories about them called *myths*. Egyptians had gods to represent many aspects of nature, as well as social roles such as motherhood. One of the Egyptian nature gods is Ra, the sun god. Ra was said to travel across the sky each day, transforming himself from a baby to an old man. Osiris was the god of plants. Isis, the wife of Osiris and mother of Horus, became the Egyptians' symbol for the ideal wife and mother.

Some gods were more important in different parts of Egypt or in different times. For example, Osiris was a minor god until the Middle Kingdom. Then he became important as the god of the underworld. Amun was the most important god in the Egyptian city of Thebes. Later he and Ra were worshipped together throughout Egypt, combined as the god Amun-Ra.

The Afterlife

The Egyptians hoped to live again after death. For this they believed the body needed to be preserved. Many modern religions say that people have souls as well as bodies. The Egyptians also believed that people were more than just bodies. They had other parts, including the ba and the ka. The *ba* is close to what we think of as the soul. In Egyptian art the ba is symbolized as a bird with a human head. The ba needed the corpse for a perch.

The *ka*, or vital force, was symbolized as two upraised arms in Egyptian painting. The ka was born at the same time as the body. When a person died, his or her ka traveled to the underworld to meet the gods. If the person's body was preserved, the ka returned to the body during the day and ate food left by the priest. It spent each night in the underworld.

The Egyptians preserved corpses by making them into mummies. This was called *embalming* (em-BOM-ing). People who were not made into mummies might be wrapped in mats or clay coffins and buried in pits with a few amulets (see About Amulets). Their families hoped their loved ones would have a good life in the afterworld.

About Amulets

Egyptians, living or dead, wore charms we call *amulets* (AM-you-lets). Egyptians believed amulets protected them from evil or gave them extra power or luck. Egyptians wore many kinds of amulets, but two were particularly popular.

Scarabs (SCARE-ubs) were figures of sacred dung beetles. The Egyptians believed dung beetles came to life magically from balls of dung (manure). They believed scarabs would help the dead person return to life. Sometimes these amulets were called heart-scarabs.

Wedjat (WEDGE-at) eyes stood for the false eye the goddess Isis gave her son Horus when his uncle Seth stole one of his eyes. Wedjat meant "healed" or "restored." Egyptians believed this eye was very powerful. They painted wedjat eyes on the sides of coffins so the corpse could look out.

Mummies

Early Egyptians mummified only royalty and high officials. In the Middle Kingdom and later, mummies were made of anyone who could afford it. There were different ways to make mummies, depending on how much the person or the family could pay.

To make the most costly mummy, a priest cut into the side of the corpse. Through the cut he removed the organs—stomach, intestines, liver, lungs—from the belly and chest. He wrapped the heart in linen and replaced it in the chest. The Egyptians believed the heart, not the brain, was the center of intelligence. The person needed it to be judged to enter the afterlife.

The priest might pull out the brain using a hook through the nose, or he might leave it in the skull.

Then the priest packed the body and some of the organs in a mound of natron and left them for weeks. The natron dried out the body and prevented rot.

When they were dry, a priest put the liver, lungs, stomach, and intestines into special stone jars called *canopic* (can-AH-pick) jars. The jars would be placed in the tomb with the coffin.

After removing the body from the natron, the priest rubbed it with oil. He packed it with sweet-smelling spices and sawdust or linen. Then he began wrapping it with linen bandages. He might use new bandages or old linen cloth. He tucked amulets into the bandages as he wrapped, saying special prayers. (See About Amulets, pages 40–41.) He wrapped each finger and toe separately. In between bandages, he might wrap the body in one or more *shrouds*, large pieces of linen that covered the body from head to toe. From time to time he painted the bandages with sticky *resin* (REZ-in), a liquid made from tree sap.

After the body was bandaged, the priest put a mask over its head. The mask was made to look like the person in life, so the person's ka would recognize the body and return to it. The mask might be made of gold or other precious metal, or it might be made of cheaper material painted gold.

Finally, the priests put the body into the coffin. Earlier coffins were wooden boxes painted with decorations and special prayers. The mummy lay on its side in these earlier coffins. Later coffins were shaped like the mummy and might be constructed of a kind of cardboard made of linen or papyrus. Sometimes the mummy was put into one coffin inside another. The coffins protected the body and made a kind of house for it.

At the funeral, professional mourners wailed and danced. Priests performed sacrifices and ceremonies. The coffin was placed in a stone *sarcophagus* (sar-KOFF-a-gus), or coffin inside the tomb. Priests made sure the corpse had everything he or she would need in the next life, including food, the person's own clothing, cosmetics, and games. Pictures or models of everyday life filled the tomb. The tomb was sealed to prevent robberies. Everything was ready for eternity.

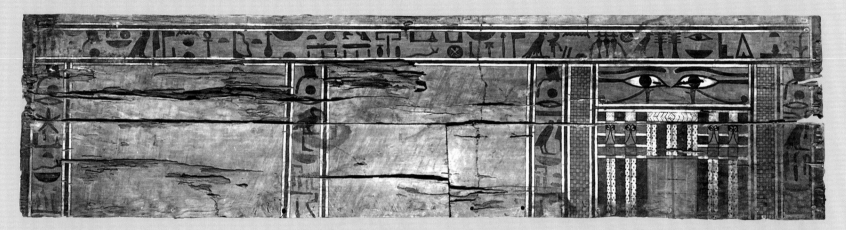

This brightly painted coffin was covered with geometric patterns and prayers. The eyes on the side let the mummy look out. Below the eyes, a painted door lets the mummy's *ka* come and go. Coffins like this were common during Egypt's Middle Kingdom. *Courtesy of Museum of Fine Arts, Boston, 04.2058, Side 1 (with ka eyes),* Coffin of the Lady of the House Neby, *Egypt, Middle Kingdom, Dynasty 12, from Beni Hasan, tomb 294, painted wood, L: 115.0 cm., H: 75.0 cm., from Garstang's excavation*

Egyptian Burial Rituals

In this activity you will make a mummy from a doll or action figure, a coffin like the ones used in the Middle Kingdom, a mummy mask, and amulets.

Materials

- ▲ Newspapers
- ▲ Shoebox with lid (if it's shiny, it may not take paint well)
- ▲ White paint
- ▲ Paintbrushes
- ▲ Jar of water
- ▲ 1 or 2 small pieces construction paper
- ▲ Fine-tipped permanent marker or pen

- ▲ Scissors
- ▲ Doll, action figure, or toy animal small enough to fit inside shoebox
- ▲ 1 roll gauze about 2 inches wide and 4 yards long
- ▲ 1 piece gold foil at least 6 by 6 inches
- ▲ Tape
- ▲ Colored markers

Directions

Spread out the newspapers. Paint the shoebox white inside and out. Paint the top and sides of the lid, too. Let them dry. (If paint won't stick to the shoebox, cover it with white paper.) Make one or more tiny amulets. Copy the wedjat eye or scarab onto a piece of construction paper about ½ inch square or you can use a photocopier to reduce the patterns shown here.

wedjat eye

Cut it out with scissors. (You can leave a small circle of construction paper around the amulet if it's hard to cut out.) Wrap the gauze completely around the doll or figurine. Tuck the amulets inside the gauze wrapping as you go. Make a mask. Draw a picture of the doll's face onto gold foil with a permanent marker. Include the ears. You can make it look Egyptian if you like. Cut it out and tape it to the front of the mummy's head. When the paint is dry, decorate the outside of the box and lid with colored

scarab

markers. Draw a pair of wedjat eyes near the mummy's face on the side of the box so the mummy can look out. Place the mummy on its side inside the coffin.

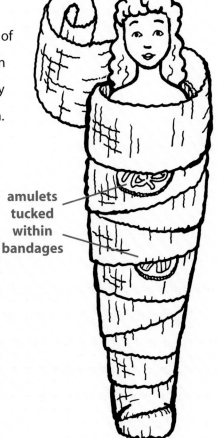

amulets tucked within bandages

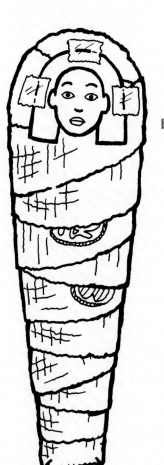

The Egyptians valued harmony and order, which they called *ma'at*. Ma'at was the name of a goddess as well as a value.

Egyptians believed it was important to lead a life of ma'at. The gods would weigh people's hearts on scales when they died. Anything a person had done that disrupted ma'at made his or her heart heavy. If the heart was heavier than a feather, the person was eaten by a monster. If the heart was lighter than the feather, the person was allowed passage to the afterlife. The feather was the symbol of the goddess Ma'at.

Conclusion

When Napoleon of France sent his troops to Egypt in 1798, he began a craze for Egyptian artifacts in the West that has lasted more than 200 years, with no signs of letting up. Egypt has influenced everything from art and architecture to furniture, fashion, and jewelry. Old movies like *The Mummy* and *Cleopatra* celebrate parts of Egyptian culture in a way that ancient Egyptians would not recognize. Stories about the "mummy's curse" or the healing power of pyramids blend East and West, ancient and modern. They do not represent ancient Egypt as it really was.

In the meantime, archaeologists have been digging up—literally—information on the real ancient Egypt. Today we know so much about Egypt's history and culture that whole books have been written just on ancient Egyptian mathematics, clothing, and astronomy.

The ancient Egyptian culture was impressively stable, lasting more than 3,000 years. You will see more change in your lifetime—at least in science—than the Egyptians experienced in 100 generations! Yet these ancient people, their love of life and their enduring creations, still bring a sense of wonder and awe. Thousands of years from now will our culture do the same?

The Mesopotamians

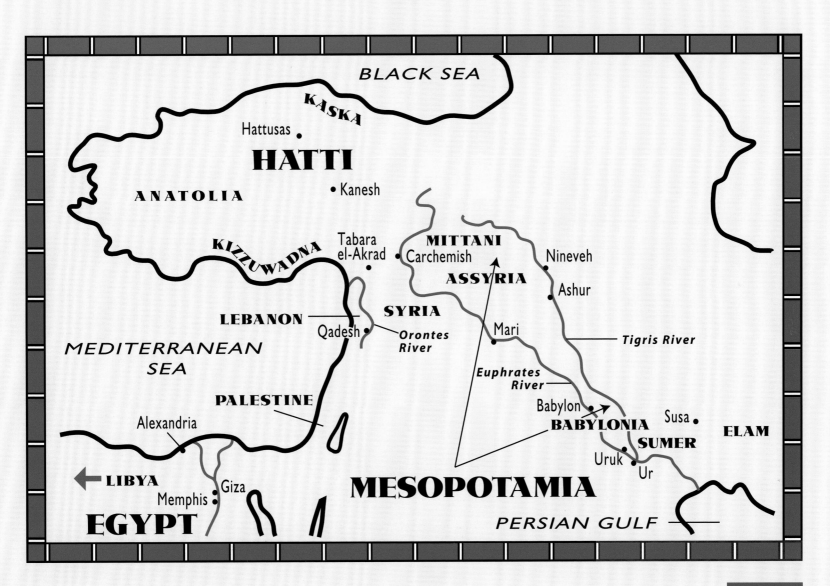

Mesopotamian History and Geography

Two mighty rivers, the Tigris (TIE-griss) and the Euphrates (you-FRAY-teze), cut across western Asia. We call the land between them *Mesopotamia*. This is Greek for "the land between two rivers."

Today the country Iraq (i-RACK) lies in southern Mesopotamia. In ancient days this dry southern part was known as Sumer (SOO-mer) or, later, Babylonia. Northern Mesopotamia—cooler and more wooded—was called Assyria (a-SEER-i-a) after its most important city, Ashur. Today, northern Mesopotamia is divided between modern Syria and Iraq.

Two cultures blended together within ancient Mesopotamia. They spoke two different languages: Sumerian and Akkadian. It's not clear just when the Sumerians and Akkadians entered Mesopotamia. Some historians believe the Sumerians arrived in Mesopotamia first. We know they were living there well before 3000 B.C. Sumerians invented writing, using the

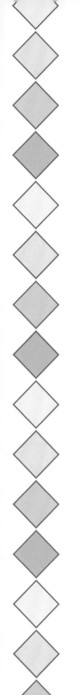

stalks of reed plants to mark clay tablets. Some scholars believe the Sumerians also invented the plow and the wheel.

Sometime before 2800 B.C., perhaps long before, people who spoke Akkadian entered the land of Sumer. Their language is related to modern Hebrew and Arabic. The Akkadian and Sumerian cultures blended into one.

The Mesopotamians built cities mentioned in the Old Testament—Nineveh, Babylon, Uruk (Erech in the Bible). They erected tall towers to the gods, called ziggurats. One of these towers may have inspired the story of the Tower of Babel (people tried to build a tower to reach heaven, and to thwart their attempt, God made each person speak a different language).

Mesopotamians made many other significant contributions. They collected the first written laws. They built magnificent palaces and irrigated their dry land with a web of canals. They wrote the first recipes on clay tablets. They created beautiful jewelry of gold, red carnelian, and blue lapis lazuli.

Historians divide Mesopotamian history into a number of periods. In the Early Dynastic Period, from about 3100 B.C. to about 2300 B.C., many Sumerian city-states (cities with their own governments that ruled over the surrounding countryside) fought for power. In the Akkadian Period, from about 2350 B.C. to about 2180 B.C., the city-states united under the Akkadian king Sargon. After his empire collapsed, the Neo-Sumerian Period began. Cities that had gone their separate ways united again under a Sumerian king. This king, Ur-Nammu, rebuilt the mighty ziggurat of Ur. He and his descendants ruled from about 2050 B.C. to about 2000 B.C.

Around the year 2000 B.C. the Sumerian king fell from power and the Old Babylonian Period began. Two city-states, Isin and Larsa, competed for power. Around

1750 B.C. the famous King Hammurabi (Ha-moo-RA-bee) of Babylon united the land. Then the Hittites raided Babylon, around 1600 B.C.

New groups came to power after the Hittites' raid on Babylon, marking the start of the Middle Babylonian Period. Foreign kings ruled Babylon, while Assyria struggled against powerful neighbors.

Around 1000 B.C. the Assyrian Empire began. The Assyrians brutally conquered many lands, including Israel. But in 612 B.C. the Babylonians, together with people called Medes, captured the Assyrian city of Nineveh, beginning the Babylonian Empire. The Babylonian Empire lasted for 73 years.

In 539 B.C., the Persian Empire began when the Persians conquered Mesopotamia. Mesopotamian culture lived on in the Persian Empire, which lasted until 330 B.C. That was the year Alexander the Great defeated Persia, beginning the Hellenistic (Greek) Period in Mesopotamia.

Mesopotamia's power was cultural as well as military. Its influence spread into ancient Greek, Roman, Arab, and Jewish cultures and from these into the modern world. Mathematics, astronomy, law, even crowns worn by European rulers—all were affected by Mesopotamian customs. Even our habit of counting time in increments of 60 comes from ancient Mesopotamia.

Mesopotamia isn't as famous in the West as ancient Egypt, Greece, and Rome. However, the women and men of ancient Mesopotamia continue to influence much of what we think, see, and do.

Mesopotamian Architecture

If you lived in a land with few trees and very little stone, what would you build with? The Mesopotamians built with something they had a lot of: mud. Their houses were made of mud bricks laid with mud mortar and covered with mud plaster. Usually their floors were mud, too. Flat roofs were made of mud-covered branches or brush. Still, parents probably told their kids, "Wipe the mud off your feet before you come inside."

To make bricks, the Mesopotamians mixed dirt with water. To keep the bricks from cracking, they added straw or sand. Then they poured this mixture into brick-shaped molds. The bricks dried in the sun. For longer-lasting bricks, they baked the bricks in ovens.

This Assyrian queen from around 900 B.C. is wearing a model of the city walls as a crown. Later, the Greeks used crowns in the same style for statues of goddesses. In the Middle Ages, European kings and queens wore similar styles. They didn't realize they were wearing models of Assyrian city walls! *Adapted from Walter Andrae,* Die Stelenreihen in Assur, *J. C. Hinrichs, 1913*

Temple Decorations

From the earliest times, Mesopotamians built beautiful temples as homes for their gods. Around 3000 B.C. people in the city of Uruk invented a wonderful way to decorate their temples. They made cones out of clay and painted the bottoms of these cones different colors. Then they pushed the cones into clay walls and columns to form designs.

One pattern the people of Uruk particularly liked was repeating triangles. They used six cones, all the same color, to make one triangle. Three cones side by side formed the base of the triangle, with the other three arranged on top in a point. Next to this triangle was an upside-down triangle in a different color. Triangles in one color alternated with upside-down triangles in another color, in a repeating pattern.

These 5,000-year-old cone mosaics covered temple pillars and walls in the ancient city of Uruk. The builders made patterns by sticking hundreds of colored cones into the wall. Left: *Courtesy of Hirmer Verlag, Munich.* Right: *Courtesy of Vorderasiatisches Museum, Staatliche Museen zu Berlin*

Mesopotamian House Model

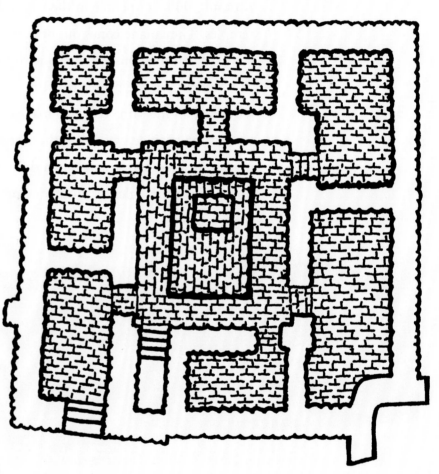

Mesopotamians built two styles of houses. In the first style, they started with several small rooms and added more rooms as needed. In the second style, they built a house around a central courtyard, which was open to the sky. Rooms opened off the courtyard. Sometimes stairs led to a second story. The roofless courtyard kept the building cool, as did the thick mud-brick walls that faced the outside. Families cooked, rested, and worked as much in the courtyard as in the rest of the house. People in the Near East still build houses in this style.

Sometimes ancient Mesopotamians buried their dead under the floors. Occasionally houses had pipes leading into these underground tombs. Families poured food and drink down the pipes to feed their ancestors.

This plan of the ground floor of a family home from Ur shows a number of rooms opening from a central courtyard. The rooms probably included a kitchen, bathroom, workroom, storage areas, religious worship room, and an entryway with steps leading to the street for greeting guests. Another staircase led to the second floor, where the family probably slept. *Adapted from* Excavations at Ur *by Sir Leonard Woolley*

Make the ground floor of a house with Legos. Follow the floor plan of an actual 4,000-year-old house from the city of Ur. The original house was two stories tall.

Materials

- ▲ *50 or more regular-size Lego pieces*
- ▲ *20 or more half-size Lego pieces*
- ▲ *Flat Lego base at least 10 inches square*
- ▲ *Scissors, tape, and a few square inches of cardboard, paper, and fabric scraps for making furnishings*

Directions

Follow the plan on page 54 to make the ground floor of a typical Mesopotamian house. Build the walls without windows.

You can make one of the rooms a storeroom and another the kitchen. Roll tiny cardboard or paper tubes to represent clay storage jars for wheat, barley, beans, and oil, and make a cardboard oven.

Make a room with an outside door as a place for greeting guests. Tape small scraps of fabric to the walls for hangings and put fabric on the floor for carpeting. In other rooms you can put tiny cardboard tables or beds, and stools made from twisted paper.

The Remains of Mesopotamian Cities

If you traveled to Mesopotamia today, you would see mounds that look like flat-topped hills dotting the countryside. The mounds are the remains of ancient cities. The mounds developed because mud dissolves in water. When the mud bricks in Mesopotamian buildings melted in the rain, people constructed new buildings on top. Gradually the ground rose higher and higher.

In ancient times, Mesopotamians built thick brick walls around the edges of the city mound for defense. These walls had turrets and gates. Important buildings like palaces and temples were inside the walls. Houses were both inside and outside. If the enemy attacked, everyone moved inside the city walls.

To see what the walls looked like, look at the picture of the crown on page 52.

Cone Mosaic

ake an attractive cone mosaic pattern like the ones on the temple walls of Uruk. Instead of clay cones, you'll use painted golf tees. Try making a pattern of repeating triangles, or invent one of your own.

Materials

▲ Newspapers
▲ Styrofoam block, at least 2 inches thick and 4 inches wide on each side. Note: A bigger block requires more tees. (Ask for the block at a florist.)
▲ 64 wooden golf tees, white or natural wood color
▲ 2 to 5 colors of tempera or acrylic paint
▲ Paintbrushes
▲ Jar of water

Directions

Spread the newspapers on the table and place the Styrofoam block on top of the newspapers.

Plan your pattern before you paint the tees. How many colors do you want? How many tees in each color?

Paint the ends of the tees and let them dry.

You'll be sticking the tees into just one side of the block. The tees are hard to rearrange once you stick them in, so plan your design first.

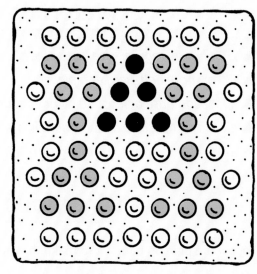

front view of finished pattern

Push the tees into the block. Be sure to leave enough room in between each of the tees so you can stick them all the way in, but don't put them so far apart you can't see the pattern.

If you like, you can paint the other sides and top of the Styrofoam block.

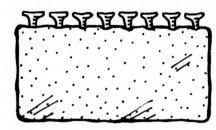

side view

Mesopotamian Clothing

In ancient Sumer, men and women made their clothes from sheepskins. Men belted sheepskins around their waists, fleece (wool) side out. Sometimes they shaved the fleece off most of the skin, leaving a fringe near the hem.

Women draped sheepskins or wool cloth around themselves to make robes or dresses. Beginning in the Old Akkadian Period men sometimes wore robes made of wool cloth, draped the same way. People often fastened their robes with a huge straight pin at the shoulder. Men usually wore the pin on the right shoulder, and women on the left.

Both men and women wore jewelry, including bracelets, necklaces, and earrings. Mesopotamian women adorned their eyes with black eyeliner made from lead.

Hairstyles

Hairstyles changed in Mesopotamia just as they do in the modern world. In the Early Dynastic Period, Sumerian men often shaved their beards and even their heads. Women wore their hair long and often pinned it up in elaborate styles. In the Old Akkadian Period, men either shaved their heads or wore their hair and beards in neat waves. Women often wore their hair in buns on the back of their heads. Sometimes they wore hairnets or hairpins made of precious metal, copper, or bone. Men and women continued to wear these styles during the Neo-Sumerian and Old Babylonian periods. During the Assyrian Empire Mesopotamian men wore luxuriantly curled hair and beards. Assyrian women wore long curled hair like the men.

Assyrian Clothing

Most Assyrians wore short-sleeved tunics under their robes. Royalty wore clothing embroidered with complicated designs and with fringed hems. Kings wore long, thickly curled hair, beards, and mustaches. Kings and queens wore earrings, necklaces, and bracelets on their wrists and upper arms. Jewelry was often made of gold inlaid with stones: turquoise, agate, and lapis lazuli.

Long Robe

Long draped robes like this one were worn by both men and women. Wear it with or without a shirt underneath. Keep your feet bare or wear sandals.

Materials

- ▲ Fabric at least 8 feet long and 3 feet wide (or ask an adult for an old twin bedsheet)
- ▲ Tape measure
- ▲ Pencil or pen
- ▲ Scissors
- ▲ 2 or 3 safety pins
- ▲ Necklaces and bracelets (optional)

The graceful folds of this robe come from a single long piece of material, worn by a Mesopotamian man around 2275 B.C. *Courtesy of Hirmer Verlag, Munich*

measure

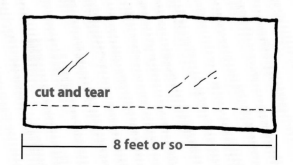

cut and tear

8 feet or so

Directions

Measure the distance between your shoulders and ankles. Measure and mark that distance on the narrow end of the fabric. Make a small cut in the fabric where you marked it, then tear it the long way. The fabric will still be 8 feet long, but is now skinnier.

Hold the fabric so the short sides go up and down. Place one end of the fabric under your left armpit. The end under the armpit should face the front. Wrap the fabric around your back and under your right armpit.

Wrap it around your front and under your left armpit again. Pin it so it's snug. Wrap the fabric once more around your back and under your right armpit. Wrap it again across your chest. Drape it over your left shoulder and pin it in front. Let the free end hang over your left shoulder and arm. You can pin the end in back for extra security.

Put on a lot of necklaces and bracelets. Heavy metal jewelry is best.

Queen's Headdress

In Ur, a city in southern Mesopotamia, royal Sumerian women wore lavish headdresses of gold and precious stones. Gold and silver leaves hung down over their foreheads. Golden flowers bobbed on top of their heads as they walked. Enormous gold earrings dangled from their earlobes.

Archaeologists found headdresses like this one on the heads of royal Sumerian women buried at Ur.

Sumerian queens and royal ladies from ancient Ur wore elaborate headdresses of precious metals, red carnelian, and blue lapis lazuli. Golden rings and leaves hung down while gold and silver flowers bobbed over their heads. *Courtesy of University of Pennsylvania Museum, negative #S8-133835*

Materials

- ▲ Thin white cardboard or poster board, at least 12 by 24 inches
- ▲ Scissors
- ▲ Newspapers
- ▲ Blue acrylic or tempera paint
- ▲ Paintbrush
- ▲ Jar of water
- ▲ 3 sheets of gold-colored foil from a craft store, at least 8$\frac{1}{2}$ by 11 inches each
- ▲ Pen or pencil
- ▲ Glue
- ▲ Stapler
- ▲ Tape

Directions

Cut a strip one to two inches wide from the long side of the cardboard. The strip must be long enough to wrap around your head, plus at least two inches for overlap. Save the rest of the cardboard.

Spread the newspapers on the table and paint the cardboard blue on one side. Let it dry.

Cut a strip of foil about two inches wide. Cut it into six to eight rectangles. Trim each rectangle into a leaf shape with a stem. Cut three large flowers out of cardboard. Don't cut out leaves or stems—just the blossoms.

Trace around the flowers onto the back of the foil. Turn the flowers over and do this again so now you have six flower tracings on the foil, three in the front and three in the back. Cut out the flower tracings and glue them to the front and back of the three cardboard flowers.

Cut a piece of cardboard at least six inches tall and three inches wide. Cut three points at the top and then cut the cardboard narrower at the end to create the flower stalk. Now trace and cut out foil to cover the front and back of this shape and glue it on. Glue a foil-covered flower to each point.

Staple the blue cardboard

leaf shapes

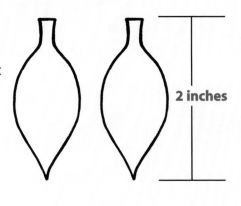

2 inches

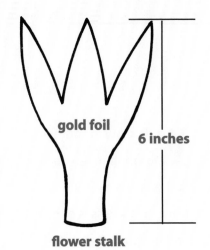

gold foil

6 inches

flower stalk

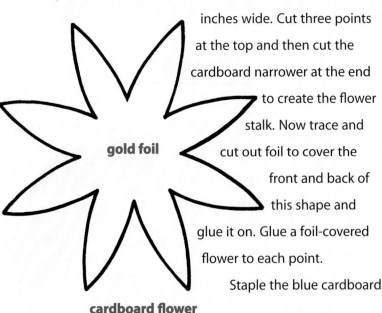

gold foil

cardboard flower

into a ring that will fit over your head with the colored side out. Use two or three staples and be sure the staple points face out. Staple the cardboard with the flowers to the back of the ring, with the flowers facing front.

Glue the stems of the gold leaves to the front of the blue ring so that the leaves hang below the cardboard.

Wear your headdress with the Mesopotamian robe and several bead necklaces.

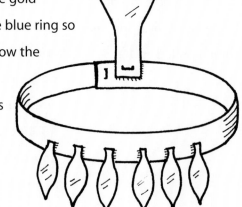

Mesopotamian Writing

For thousands of years before the time of this book begins (3100 B.C.), people in the ancient Near East couldn't write—but they did keep records. The first record keeping wasn't like anything we call writing today. People made clay pieces to stand for goods that were traded or brought to temples as offerings. One shape stood for a sheep. Another shape stood for a measure of grain. Other shapes stood for oil and more animals. Countries many miles apart used the same shapes, showing that ancient people traveled and traded a great deal.

After thousands of years of this system, people began putting the clay pieces inside a clay ball to show how many sheep or measures of grain were given or traded or sold at one time. Because they couldn't see what was inside, they scratched or pressed marks on the surface of the ball to show what pieces were hidden within. Then a clever scribe realized if he marked the surface of the balls, he didn't need pieces inside. He didn't even need a ball! The result was the beginning of writing.

By the time this book starts, the Sumerians had invented writing. They no longer used the clay balls or pieces at all. Instead they used symbols like the ones they had scratched on the surface of the balls. They drew these symbols on wet clay slabs, called *tablets*, with the stem of a reed plant. This was the first writing.

At first the Mesopotamians wrote by drawing pictures. But drawing curved lines in clay is tricky—so they found a way to make pictures without curves. They noticed that pressing the end of a reed stem into wet clay made a wedge shape. They combined many wedge shapes into a single picture. Today we call wedge-writing *cuneiform* (KYOON-ee-i-form), which means "wedge-shaped" in Latin.

From Pictures to Sounds

Not every word can be easily shown with a picture. The Sumerians realized this. They began using symbols to stand for sounds as well as words. Their word for sky was *An*. They showed the word by making a sign like a star. After a while they used that same sign for any word that had the sound *an* in it. Signs sometimes stood for syllables, and sometimes for entire words.

The Sumerians invented writing about 3300 B.C.—two hundred years before the start of this book, and about two hundred years before the Egyptians began to use hieroglyphic symbols to write.

People who spoke Akkadian learned to write from the Sumerians. They used the same signs for their own language and developed new ones. Other cultures, including the Hittites, learned cuneiform from the Mesopotamians. They, too, used cuneiform to form their own language. There are even ancient clay dictionaries showing the same word in three or four languages—all written in cuneiform!

Seals and Sealing

Mesopotamians, like other people in the ancient Near East, used objects called *seals* to stamp or roll symbols onto clay. They used the seal to sign letters written on clay or to mark their property. At first kings and officials were the only ones to have their own seals. Later, wealthy men and women, and sometimes ordinary people, owned them.

The Mesopotamians invented *cylinder seals*. Cylinder seals were shaped like short fat tubes. They were usually made of stone, or sometimes metal or baked clay. Special crafts-people engraved the seal with words or pictures. When the seal was rolled across wet clay, a design appeared on the clay. The seal was usually pierced (like a tube or bead) so the owner could put it on a cord or pin. People often wore seals as jewelry.

Most seals showed pictures of gods and humans. Often the name of the owner was written in cuneiform on the seal—backward. That way the name would come out correctly when the seal was rolled across clay.

In those days when most people couldn't write, cylinder seals acted like signatures. They were rolled across letters or legal documents. They could also be used to protect the contents of jars, boxes, or rooms. A lump of clay was pressed against cloth that covered the neck of a jar or the handle on a door. The seal was rolled across the clay. Once the clay dried, if anyone tried to get into the jar or the room, the clay and seal would crack. So someone buying a jar of wine with an intact seal could be sure no one had opened it since the seal was put on.

Cylinder seals left personal marks in the days before signatures. When the cylinder seal at the left was rolled across moist clay, it created the picture on the right. *From* Das wiedererstehende Babylon *by Robert Koldewey*

Cylinder Seal

Make your own personal seal like the ancient Mesopotamians. You can use it to make clay name tags or place cards. You can also pierce it and wear it as jewelry.

Adult help recommended with the wire and the oven.

Materials

- ▲ 1 block polymer clay such as Sculpey or Fimo, in 1 or more colors
- ▲ 8-inch length of heavy wire, such as the straight part of a coat hanger
- ▲ Plastic knife
- ▲ Scissors
- ▲ Sheet of typing paper
- ▲ Marker
- ▲ Pencil
- ▲ Oven-proof bowl
- ▲ Oven
- ▲ Potholders
- ▲ Toothpicks
- ▲ 12-inch length of thin cord

Directions

Preheat the oven according to the directions on the clay.

Using half of the clay block, knead it and roll it into a fat cylinder one to two inches long. You can knead several colors together if you like.

Using the wire, pierce the middle of the cylinder from one end to the other. Twist the wire so the hole gets bigger. Leave the wire inside and move the clay to the center of the wire. Use the plastic knife to trim the ends of the cylinder.

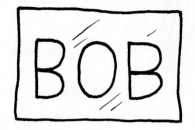

Cut a one by two-inch piece from the typing paper. Using a thin marker, write your name on it in big letters. Turn the paper

over so your name appears backward. Scratch your name backward onto the cylinder with the pencil. Dig out the letters so they are wide and deep. You can carve your name along the length of the cylinder or around it—or even diagonally. Carve other decorations if you like. Whatever you carve out will show up as a raised area when you use the seal.

Lay the wire across the rim of the bowl so that the cylinder is suspended in the middle of it. Bake according to the directions on the clay.

When the clay is done, remove the bowl from the oven with potholders and let it cool. Slide the seal off the wire. Remember to turn off the oven.

Form the rest of the clay into a flat rectangle. It should be wider than your seal. Roll your seal across the clay. Use the knife to cut

apart and trim each impression of your name. Once the clay is dry, you can use these tags as name tags for your desk or room or as your place card at the dinner table. Be sure to clean your seal with a toothpick after using it, while the clay is still moist.

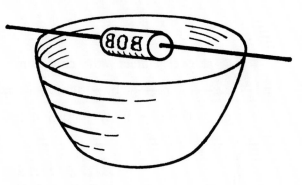

To wear your seal, push the cord through the hole and tie it around your neck.

Clay Letter and Envelope

Make a clay tablet with a cuneiform greeting. Guard your secret message by putting your clay letter into a clay envelope. Allow several days for drying.

Materials

- ▲ ¼ cup self-hardening clay such as Marblex, or ordinary potter's clay
- ▲ Plastic bag or airtight container
- ▲ Damp cloth
- ▲ Old pencil
- ▲ Cylinder seal or rubber stamp (optional)

Directions

Making the Letter

Put half the clay in a plastic bag or airtight container with a damp cloth to keep it moist. Knead the rest. Make a square or rectangle two to three inches on a side, shaped like a flat pillow. It should be wider than your cylinder seal or stamp. Smooth the front and back for writing.

With the pencil or clay tool, write the words *ana shulmanim* on one side of the tablet. Ana shulmanim means "greeting" in Akkadian, one of the languages of Mesopotamia. (In reality, the Mesopotamians used cuneiform, not our alphabet, to write the word.)

Let your tablet dry an hour or so until it's somewhat hard. Turn it over. Roll your cylinder seal carefully across the blank side.

front   **back**

Let your tablet dry completely before making the envelope.

Making the Envelope

Knead and flatten the remaining clay. Wrap it all the way around the dry clay letter, so no part of the letter shows. Smooth the clay.

Roll your cylinder seal across the envelope, or stamp it with the rubber stamp.

Remember to clean the seal or stamp afterward.

Let the envelope dry. Someday, give it to someone for a surprise and tell her to break off the envelope.

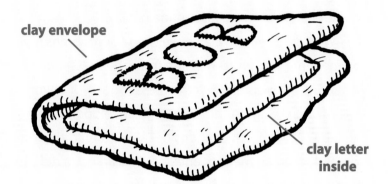

clay envelope

clay letter inside

Mesopotamian Mail

The Mesopotamians sent each other letters written on clay tablets. Without a post office, they had to entrust the letters to messengers or to travelers who were going in the right direction. They would often put the letters into envelopes, which were also made of clay.

Why did they use clay envelopes? Sometimes it was to hide what was written inside from the messenger. Other times, it was to keep the messenger—or anyone else—from changing the letter. The envelope protected the letter inside from changes because to read the letter, you had to break the clay envelope. As an extra defense, the scribe might write the entire letter over again on the envelope. When the letter was delivered, the person who got it could compare the writing on the envelope with the writing on the letter. If there were any differences, he could blame the messenger.

Assyrians living in an Assyrian trading colony in Anatolia sent clay letters inside clay envelopes to people back home. You can see that a cylinder seal was used to mark the envelope. *Courtesy of Museum of Anatolian Civilizations, Ankara*

Mesopotamian Work

Ancient Mesopotamia was a complex society. Most people worked in agriculture, but people did many other kinds of work as well. The government or the temples employed people as officials, priests, or priestesses. Even farmers or shepherds might work for a temple, raising grain or goats to be eaten by the priests or offered to a god.

Other Mesopotamians worked as craftspeople making jewelry, pottery, furniture, or cloth. They might make their goods for the temple or the palace, or sell their goods to other Mesopotamians. Often they traded their goods to merchants, who took them to other countries for sale. Other times they created things for their own use.

Weaving on a Hanging Loom

Mesopotamians wove two kinds of cloth: wool and linen. They spun the fibers into thread, then wove the thread into cloth. Most often women did the weaving.

Mesopotamians made cloth to sell, as well as for their own families. They usually wove in their own homes, but archaeologists have discovered ancient weaving workshops that employed thousands of people.

Mesopotamians used different kinds of looms. A common type of loom hung thread vertically (up and down). Weavers tied weights at the end of the vertical threads to keep them taut.

You can make a belt of weaving with a hanging loom.

Adult help recommended in making and threading the loom.

Materials

▲ *1 or 2 colors of wool or acrylic yarn (regular weight, not extra fine); 104 yards for a belt; 52 yards for a hanging*

▲ *Scissors*

▲ *1 chopstick (any kind)*

▲ *7 large metal nuts or large beads, wide enough to slide onto the chopstick*

▲ *8 metal washers (steel is best)*

▲ *1 Styrofoam tray at least 8 inches long. Ask for one at the grocery meat counter.*

▲ *Door with doorknob (or other place to hang loom while weaving). To make a belt, you also need another higher spot to hang the loom.*

▲ *1 bobby pin*

Directions

Making and Threading the Loom

Cut eight equal lengths of yarn. For a belt, cut each length 4$\frac{1}{2}$ feet long; for a hanging, cut each length 18 inches long.

Slide all the metal nuts or beads onto the chopstick. Make sure they are loose enough to slide back and forth. Tie the end of a length of yarn to the chopstick just before the first nut. Now tie

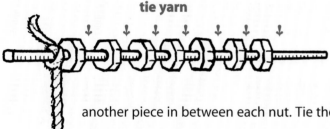

tie yarn

another piece in between each nut. Tie the last piece just past the last nut. You will wind up with yarn, nut, yarn, nut, and so on, ending with yarn. Slide the nuts and yarn around so there are no spaces in between. Tighten your knots.

Tie a washer onto each piece of yarn. If you are making a hanging, tie the washer at the end of each piece. If you're making a belt, tie the washers about one foot from the chopstick.

From the flat middle part of

the meat tray, cut a piece about 6 inches by 1$\frac{1}{2}$ inches. In the middle of one long side, make eight cuts, $\frac{1}{2}$ inch apart and about $\frac{1}{2}$ inch deep. Save the rest of the Styrofoam: you may need to replace this piece if it breaks.

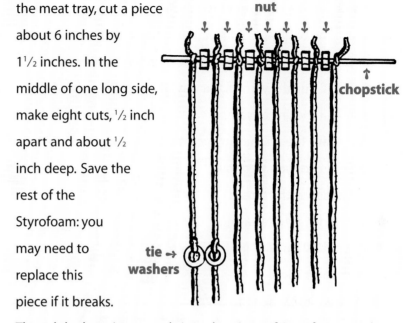

nut

chopstick

tie washers

Thread the hanging strands into the piece of Styrofoam one by one. Push the Styrofoam a few inches from the chopstick.

Cut one more piece of yarn about two feet long. Tie it securely to each end of the chopstick. Use this to hang the loom from the doorknob.

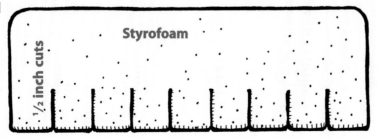

Styrofoam

$\frac{1}{2}$ inch cuts

Weaving

Cut a piece of yarn about a yard long. Thread it through the "eye," or closed end, of the bobby pin. To keep this weaving yarn secure, tie one end of it to the chopstick near the last nut. Starting at that side, weave the bobby pin with yarn under and over the hanging threads just under the chopstick. Weave under one thread and over the next. Pull the yarn all the way through. With your fingers, even out the line of yarn.

Now, weave the bobby pin back the other way. This time go under the threads you went over last time, and over the threads you went under. After weaving each row, push it up with the Styrofoam so it's even.

Keep weaving. When the yarn you are weaving with nearly runs out, tie on

another piece. To make stripes, wait until the end of several rows, cut your weaving yarn (leaving an extra 3 inches), then tie on a different color. Trim the ends with scissors.

If you need your doorknob back, unhook the loom and put it gently in a box or bag. If you are making a belt, your weaving will get too long to hang from a doorknob. You will need to find someplace higher to hang it from. Try a lampstand (with lamp turned off) or curtain rod. You will also need to untie the washers and lower them.

When you have woven all you can, remove the Styrofoam piece and the washers. Tie the weaving thread to the last horizontal thread. Tie each hanging thread to the one next to it, so you have pairs of threads knotted together in four knots right at the edge of the fabric. Tie the extra thread to the knot next to it. Leave a fringe.

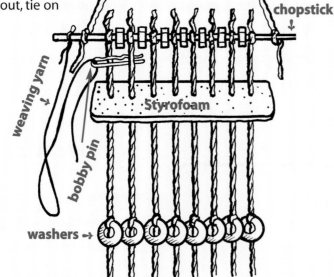

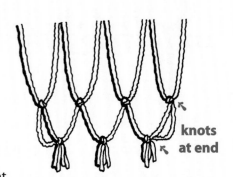

Untie or slide off the yarn hanger. Slide the knotted ends off the chopstick two at a time (also removing the nuts or beads.) Tie each thread to the one next to it as you did at the other end. Tie the extra thread to the knot next to it.

Trim the fringes on the two ends so they're even. Beautiful!

Medicine

In the ancient world, people got sick just as they do today—possibly sicker! If you lived in Babylonia, you might have come down with a *nishu* or a *guhhu*. A nishu was a cold, a guhhu was a cough, and if your guhhu was very bad you might need to *hahu ru'uti*, or spit saliva. Try saying those words out loud. Pronounce the "h" in the back of your throat, like "ch" in the German word *ach*. Don't they sound like what they're describing?

There were several kinds of people who treated illness in Babylonia. If you got sick, your family might call in an *asu*, a man or woman who would treat you with salves or potions concocted of herbs and minerals. Or, instead, they might call in a man called an *ashipu*. An ashipu would tell you what was causing your illness: perhaps a ghost or demon, or the "hand of a god." He would then perform rituals or recite prayers to make you well. In one treatment, the ashipu took the beak of a black raven, stitched it up in a leather purse, and placed it around the patient's neck.

Often families called in both an asu and an ashipu, and sometimes a *mashmushu* as well. A mashmushu was an exorcist. If the ashipu couldn't manage to chase away the demon making you sick, perhaps the mashmushu could.

People often did get better after this treatment. Of course, they might have gotten better even without it.

Math Sumerian-Style

Keeping track of trade and temple offerings was critical. Mesopotamians needed a system of math to be able to do this. The Sumerians invented the use of clay shapes on a counting board. The shapes stood for different numbers: 1, 10, 60, 600, and higher.

The words the Sumerians used to solve math problems were different from ours. When they multiplied 3 by 3, they called it, "letting 3 eat with 3." They solved complex problems using this system of math. Mesopotamians used math in buying, selling, planning buildings, and measuring land.

Surprise your teacher by adding, subtracting, and multiplying like the ancient Sumerians. Instead of clay shapes, you can use paper clips, toothpicks, and rubber bands.

Materials

▲ Tray, large box lid, or large piece of paper for a counting board
▲ 20 toothpicks. Each toothpick stands for 1.
▲ 10 large paper clips. Each paper clip stands for 10 toothpicks.
▲ 10 thick rubber bands. Each rubber band stands for 6 paper clips or 60 toothpicks.

Directions

Try making different numbers on your counting board. Set out:

6 (Use six toothpicks.)

13 (One paper clip and three toothpicks.)

47 (Four paper clips and seven toothpicks.)

65 (One rubber band and five toothpicks. Remember, six paper clips are the same as one rubber band.)

To add, place the objects representing the two numbers to be added on the counting board. If you end up with 10 toothpicks, replace them with a paper clip. If you end up with six paper clips, replace them with one rubber band.

Try adding:

Add 5 and 7.

Lay out five tooth-picks and seven more toothpicks.

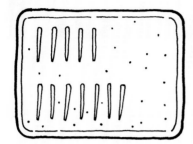

lay out 5

lay out 7

Replace ten toothpicks with a paper clip.

Read your result: one paper clip (10) plus two toothpicks

(2) = 12.

Now try adding different numbers, such as 8 and 35; 12 and 53; 13 and 65.

Replace 10 with a paper clip.

You can multiply as well. To multiply 2 x 3, lay two toothpicks above the top of the counting board (not on it). Now underneath each toothpick, put three more toothpicks—but put these on the counting board. You end up with six toothpicks on the board. That's your answer.

Try multiplying:

5 x 3 (You will end up with one paper clip and five toothpicks.)

6 x 5

Now let seven eat with seven. That means, multiply 7 x 7.

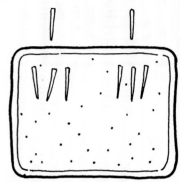

Count toothpicks on the board for the total.

Mesopotamian Food

What did people in ancient Mesopotamia eat? Like other ancient people, they ate a lot of bread. They baked bread from an ancient wheat called emmer or from barley flour. Some of their bread was flat with a pocket inside, like the pita bread eaten in the Near East today.

Mesopotamians ate many different kinds of food. They used cow's milk for cheese and other dairy foods. They dried fish and pressed them into blocks, then cut off the amount they wanted. Sometimes they made a fish sauce called *shiqqu* (SHEEK-koo). At weddings and other special occasions, they ate meat such as lamb, deer, goat, duck, or goose. The Babylonians also enjoyed eating a kind of mouse.

Mesopotamians were lucky enough to enjoy a variety of fruits, including apples, pears, dates, grapes, figs, and pomegranates. They ate onions, garlic, lettuce, cucumbers, and mushrooms, too. For flavoring, they used many herbs and spices, including mint, rue, rosemary, and coriander—even pieces of fragrant wood. They sweetened foods with honey and date sugar and pressed oil from sesame seeds, olives, and flax. A special delicacy was pickled grasshoppers served on long sticks, or skewers.

Poor people, such as laborers, had less variety in their diet. Sometimes poor people lived mostly on bread and onions. They ate onions raw, like apples.

Astoundingly, scholars have found actual Mesopotamian recipes written on clay tablets. These recipes—for soups, stews, and bird pies—may well be 3,700 years old! Some of these recipes sound amazingly modern, although certain ingredients are unfamiliar to us. Since ordinary people couldn't read, the recipes were probably for temple or palace use.

In one recipe for bird pie, the cook sprinkles small birds with salt and cooks them in a pot with water, milk, fat, and seasonings. Meanwhile, the cook makes dough from *sasku* flour, milk, garlic, leek (a vegetable like an onion), fish sauce, and other ingredients. The cook makes the dough into a piecrust and also into *sebetu* (seh-BAY-too) rolls. While the birds cook, the piecrust and rolls bake. Finally, the cook puts the birds and the rolls together inside the crusts for a pie.

Sebetu Rolls

You can make sebetu rolls based on an actual 3,700-year-old recipe. This is a modern version of sebetu rolls. Some of the ingredients have been left out or changed. For instance, the original recipe calls for sasku flour. Since we don't know what this is, this recipe uses regular flour. Instead of fish sauce, this version uses salted water. This version also calls for baking powder.

You can add these to soup as dumplings.

Adult help recommended with the oven.

Utensils

- ▲ Oven
- ▲ Baking sheet
- ▲ Paper towel
- ▲ Measuring cups
- ▲ Large mixing bowl
- ▲ Measuring spoons
- ▲ Large spoon for stirring
- ▲ Small mixing bowl
- ▲ Garlic press
- ▲ Rubber spatula
- ▲ Timer or clock
- ▲ Potholders
- ▲ Spatula
- ▲ Plate

Ingredients

- ▲ 3 teaspoons oil
- ▲ 1 cup flour
- ▲ 1½ teaspoons baking powder
- ▲ ¼ teaspoon salt
- ▲ 2 tablespoons water
- ▲ ¼ cup milk
- ▲ 1 garlic clove
- ▲ 2 scallions, white part only (optional)

Directions

Preheat oven to 400°.

Pour one teaspoon oil onto the baking sheet. Spread it evenly with the paper towel.

Scoop the flour into the large mixing bowl. Add the baking powder and mix it with the flour. Set this bowl aside.

In the smaller mixing bowl, stir together the water and salt. Add the milk and stir. Add two teaspoons oil to the milk and water mixture, and stir.

Peel the garlic clove and crush it with the garlic press. Be sure to scrape the crushed garlic off the back of the press and into the small bowl. Throw away what's left inside the press.

Crush the white bulbs of the scallions with the garlic press the same way. Add to the small bowl and stir.

Pour the wet ingredients into the large bowl with the flour, and stir.

With clean hands, knead the dough inside the large bowl. Scrape the sides with the rubber spatula and knead again.

Shape the dough into about eight to ten rolls and put them on the baking sheet. Put the sheet in the oven.

Set the timer for 15 minutes. Look at the rolls after that time. If they are golden brown, remove the pan from the oven with potholders. If they are just beginning to brown, keep baking. Check every two minutes.

Remove the rolls from the baking sheet with the spatula. Let them cool on the plate for a few minutes. Remember to turn off the oven. Serve warm.

A Royal Assyrian Meal

Play the part of a king, queen, or servant at a royal Assyrian feast. You need at least two people—one to be a servant and one to be a king or queen. Take turns playing the servant.

Materials

▲ 1 chair for each royal diner

▲ 1 small table

▲ Fresh apples, pears, or grapes

▲ Dried dates or figs

▲ Sebetu rolls, if you made them

▲ 1 small bowl for each royal diner

▲ Apple or grape juice

▲ 1 tray or plate for each servant

▲ 1 fan for each servant to carry (use a folded newspaper or feather duster)

Directions

Royal diners sit on chairs or lie on the sofa with the small table nearby. Meanwhile, servants arrange the food on plates or trays, pour juice into each small bowl, and bring one bowl to each royal person. Servants should walk very slowly with good posture. Next, servants carry in the fruit and rolls. Following this tray of food, they carry in a fan. After putting the trays on the table, the servants fan the diners while they eat.

Royal diners should sit up to drink. The king or queen on the sofa should lean on cushions but keep his or her feet on the sofa.

Assyrian Feasts

Ashurbanipal (ah-shur-BAN-i-pal), an Assyrian king, recorded what he served at a banquet to celebrate his luxurious new palace, the "joy of his heart." At this feast, to which he invited the god Ashur and all the other gods of the land, he claims he served:

14,000	ordinary sheep from the flocks belonging to the goddess Ishtar	1,000	lambs	1,000	large birds	10,000	eggs
		1,000	young cattle and sheep from the stalls	500	geese	10,000	loaves of bread
				10,000	doves	10,000	measures of beer
				10,000	small birds		
1,000	fattened sheep	500	game birds	2,500	other birds	10,000	measures of wine
1,000	barley-fed oxen	500	gazelles	10,000	fish		

And that's not even the entire menu! Presumably some human beings shared this meal with the gods.

King Ashurbanipal of Assyria and his queen feast in a garden in the 7th century B.C. *Copyright The British Museum, London*

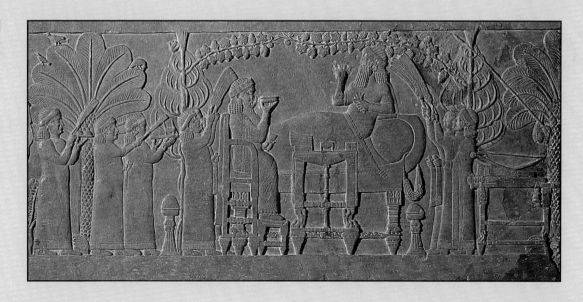

Mesopotamian Religion

The Mesopotamians—like the Egyptians and the Hittites—believed that gods and goddesses were responsible for everything that happened in the world. Each god had specific areas he or she was responsible for, such as love or justice. Sometimes these areas changed over time.

Gods and goddesses had jobs that affected the world in general. They also watched over individual towns, cities, and people. Every Mesopotamian had his or her own protective god or goddess. Every village, town, and city had its own protector as well.

Early Mesopotamian gods had Sumerian names. Later, some were given Akkadian names. At times they were called by both. Here are a few names of gods and goddesses and their jobs.

God or Goddess	Sumerian Name	Akkadian Name	Job Responsibilities
Planet Venus	Inanna	Ishtar	love and war
Sun God	Utu	Shamash	justice
Moon God	Nanna	Suen	time reckoning
Storm God	Ishkur	Adad	thunder and rain

The gods expected people to sacrifice animals and follow rituals to keep them happy. Special priests and priestesses washed and dressed images of the god every day, scenting them with perfume and draping them with jewels. The priests burned food offerings and served them meals. They played music and lit incense for them.

If the gods were happy, they did their jobs—they made plants grow and people thrive. If the gods were angry, they punished the people. They caused famines, illness, or losses in battle.

If something bad happened, such as a drought, special priests and priestesses had to figure out what the people had done wrong. Mesopotamians believed gods passed messages to people many different ways, including through dreams, changes in the weather or the stars, or other signs. All that the priests had to do was interpret these messages. They kept long lists on clay tablets of what different signs could mean.

One common way the priests used to read the gods' messages was by looking at sheep livers. During a drought, a priest might sacrifice a sheep. Another priest, called a *baru*, who could be a man or a woman, would look at its liver. The baru would study the liver

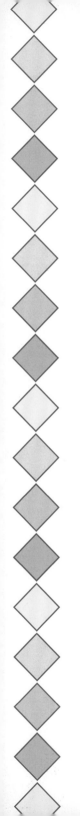

for anything unusual in its shape or its blood vessels, or any other features that made it different from other livers. Then he or she would explain what these findings meant.

Mesopotamians thought liver shapes were so important they called them the "writing of the gods." They used this phrase to refer to the patterns of the stars as well. Mesopotamians believed that if you knew how to interpret these signs, you could read the will of the gods as easily as a clay tablet.

A Substitute King

Priests believed that by studying sheep livers, strange events, or changes in the stars, they could predict the future. Kings and wealthy people would ask for *oracles*, or predictions, before they went into battle, started to build a new palace, or other major events. These oracles told them the gods' plans for the future.

Even if something bad was predicted, that didn't necessarily mean it would come true, according to the priests. The gods and goddesses could be tricked or persuaded to take some other action.

Sometimes priests in Mesopotamia interpreted signs in the heavens or other events to mean the king was going to die. When this happened, they protected the king from the gods by turning an ordinary man, such as a gardener, into a substitute king. This ordinary person was dressed in the king's robe and crown and sent to live in the king's palace. He sat on the throne, met with courtiers and officials, and pretended to make decisions. Meanwhile, the king moved into a quiet room nearby. Those around him called him a farmer instead of a king. In fact, the real king quietly kept on ruling the country. When the danger period ended, the substitute king was executed and buried. The real king returned to the throne.

This figurine of King Ur-Nammu shows him carrying a basket of clay on his head. The clay was to make the first brick to rebuild the temple to Enlil, chief god of ancient Sumer. This figurine of the king was buried in a box under one of the temple towers along with beads and a stone tablet. Kings often left figurines and written records like this buried under temples they had built.
Courtesy of the Oriental Institute Museum

Ziggurat

Every city had its special god, and every city had a special temple for that god. Near the main temple in most cities was a giant staircase to heaven called a *ziggurat*. Ziggurats looked a lot like pyramids—especially the step pyramid. But, unlike pyramids, ziggurats were not tombs—they were resting places for the gods as they came down to earth. Ziggurats had three to seven levels with a shrine (tiny temple) at the top where the god could rest. Mesopotamians believed that the god would descend from heaven, rest at the top of the ziggurat, then come down to visit his or her temple. Ziggurats also had regular stair-cases so priests, priestesses, and temple servants could climb to the top. Ziggurats required millions of clay bricks. Sometimes the bricks were covered with paint or tiles to make the levels different colors.

You can still see remains of some ziggurats in Iraq. The most famous ziggurats were in the cities of Babylon and Ur.

King Ur-Nammu built this ziggurat in Ur around 2100 B.C. Baked clay bricks surrounded a solid center of unbaked brick. The ziggurat was dedicated to the city's main goddess or god. *By permission of Oxford University Press*, Ur Excavations, Volume V: The Ziggurat and Its Surroundings, *by Sir Leonard Woolley*

Model Ziggurat—Staircase for a God

You can make a ziggurat modeled on one built by King Ur-Nammu about 2100 B.C. This ziggurat was in the ancient city of Ur. You'll make your own clay as part of this activity. Allow two or three days for drying.

Adult help recommended with the stove.

Materials

- 4 thin, empty boxes:
  1 large, like a cereal box
  1 medium, like a cornstarch box
  1 small, like a baking soda box
  1 tiny, like a small matchbox or jewelry box
- Newspapers (3 or 4 daily papers' worth)
- Scissors
- Duct tape or masking tape
- Wooden board at least 3 inches wider and 2 inches longer than the largest box
- Glue
- Clean piece of paper
- Fat book or other heavy object

Artificial Clay Ingredients

- Medium-sized pot
- 1 cup cornstarch
- 2 cups baking soda
- 1¼ cups warm water
- Spoon for stirring
- Stove
- Potholder
- Large plate
- Plastic knife
- Tempera or acrylic paints
- Paintbrushes
- Jar of water

Directions

Fill each of the four boxes with old newspapers. Try to make the boxes firm but not bulging. Try trimming the newspapers and stuffing them in whole, rather than crumpling them. Tape each box closed.

Glue the largest box to the middle of the board.

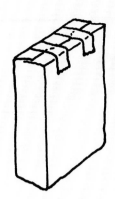

Glue the medium box on top of the largest box. Glue the next-smallest box on top of the medium box. (Save the tiniest box for later.) Put a clean piece of paper on the very top and gently balance a heavy object on it to help the glue set. Leave it for at least 30 minutes.

Meanwhile, make artificial clay. You will have to use the clay within 30 minutes after you make it.

Mix the cornstarch and baking soda in the pot. Add warm water and stir. Cook it over medium heat, stirring constantly. Use a potholder if the pot handle gets hot. The mixture will boil, then begin to get thick. Keep stirring. When it is as thick as mashed potatoes, scoop it onto a plate to cool. Remember to turn off the stove.

While the clay cools, remove the heavy object and paper from the top of the ziggurat and glue on the smallest box.

book
↓

board

Once the clay has cooled, use it to make sloping wedges from level to level (for staircases). Make two long sloping staircases out to the sides, in front.

Shape other trimmings as you like: a dome over the front staircase, or side buildings on some of the levels. Hint: you can use the plastic knife to cut straight sides and tops.

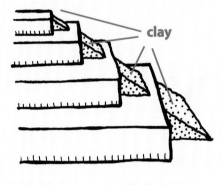

clay

side view sample staircases

Let the ziggurat dry overnight. When it's completely dry, paint it. Try painting the different levels of the ziggurat different bright colors (blue, white, yellow, green, or others). When the paint is completely dry (maybe an hour, depending on the paint), add a second coat.

Quick and Sweet Ziggurat You can also make a great ziggurat out of sugar cubes, like the pyramid in the Egyptian section. Make each level rectangular instead of square, and cut cubes diagonally in half to make staircases. (Adult help recommended if using a sharp knife.)

Conclusion

Most of us don't realize how much ancient Mesopotamia has influenced our lives. People talk much more about Rome and Greece—but those cultures borrowed many ideas from Mesopotamia. A Greek named Pythagoras gets credit for a mathematical idea—but the Mesopotamians used that idea a thousand years before. The Mesopotamians were the first to chart the stars, the first to write stories, and even the first to make personal horoscopes. Most importantly, the Mesopotamians invented writing. They wrote so much that we know details of the lives of students who lived thousands of years ago: where they lived, what they studied, what kind of presents they wanted from their parents (new clothes). Thousands of Mesopotamian tablets are still waiting to be translated. Who knows what we will learn from these.

The Nubians

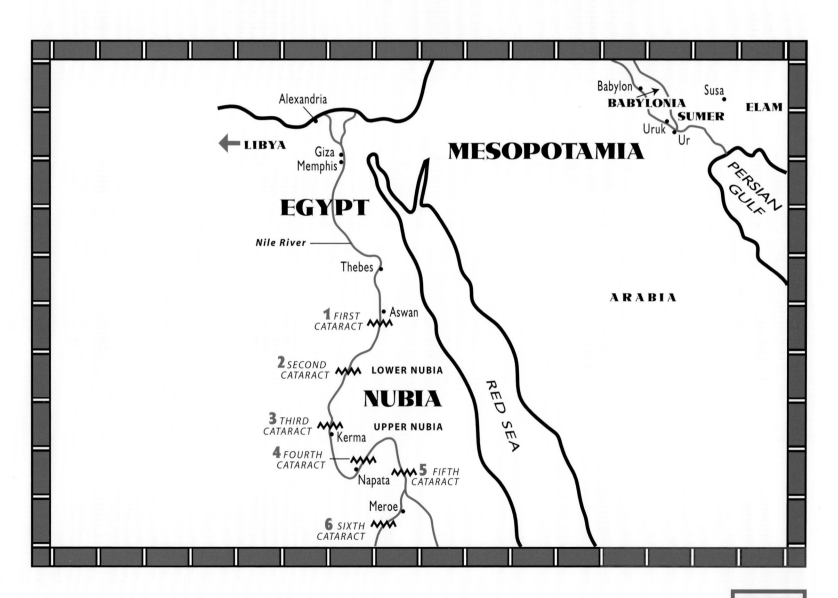

- Alexandria
- LIBYA
- Giza
- Memphis
- **EGYPT**
- Nile River
- Thebes
- **1** *FIRST CATARACT* — Aswan
- **2** *SECOND CATARACT* — LOWER NUBIA
- **NUBIA**
- **3** *THIRD CATARACT* — Kerma
- UPPER NUBIA
- **4** *FOURTH CATARACT*
- **5** *FIFTH CATARACT* — Napata
- Meroe
- **6** *SIXTH CATARACT*
- **MESOPOTAMIA**
- Babylon
- **BABYLONIA**
- Susa
- **ELAM**
- Uruk
- **SUMER**
- Ur
- PERSIAN GULF
- **ARABIA**
- RED SEA

Nubian History and Geography

In ancient times, the banks of the Nile River were home to two different cultures. The Nubians lived along the Nile to the south. The Egyptians lived along the Nile to the north. Generally, the farther south along the Nile people lived, the darker their skins. The Nubians usually had darker skins than the Egyptians. However, many Egyptians had fairly dark skin as well.

Nubia is a dry and harsh land. A number of rocky rapids and waterfalls, called *cataracts*, break up the flow of the Nile as it passes through Nubia. The First Cataract is at a town called Aswan today. In ancient times, Aswan served as the border between Egypt and Nubia.

The land that was ancient Nubia is divided today between two countries. Most of it is in the Sudan. The northernmost part is in modern Egypt. Today the area is still called Nubia, even if it is no longer a separate country. Ancient Egyptians, and perhaps ancient Nubians as well, called it Kush.

Ancient Nubia shared many customs with Egypt. Most Nubians, like Egyptians, lived by farming the land irrigated by the Nile's floods or by raising livestock. They grew

Nubia Underwater

In 1960, the Egyptians began building a high dam at Aswan. They knew that when it was finished, the dam would create a lake flooding most of northern Nubia. Ancient ruins that had never been studied would disappear forever underwater in a few short years.

Egypt and the Sudan invited archaeologists from the entire world to study these ancient settlements quickly and many countries participated throughout the early 1960s. Archaeologists dug up towns and graves belonging to A-Group and C-Group Nubians along with artifacts from other periods. They enriched the world's knowledge of ancient Nubian lives. They moved massive stone monuments to safety, first cutting them into pieces with a thin saw, then transporting them by boat to new positions in Egypt or the Sudan. Under an agreement with Egypt and the Sudan, archaeologists were allowed to take half of what they uncovered to their home countries. The Temple of Dendur from the west bank of the Nubian Nile now greets visitors to the Metropolitan Museum of Art in New York.

Today the ancient settlements of Lower Nubia are covered by a lake. Researchers can still study Nubian settlements farther south, but the ones under the lake are covered forever.

With much sadness, in 1963 and 1964, the Nubian people who lived in the area that was flooded moved to Egypt and the Sudan. Their families had lived in Nubia for generations, some for centuries.

emmer wheat and barley and a grain called millet, and kept sheep, goats, and cattle. But farming was harder in Nubia. The strips of land watered by the Nile were narrower than in Egypt, and in many places the desert reached all the way to the river. Even so, this harsh land was the beloved home of the Nubian people.

Egypt was a single unified country for most of its history. Nubia, however, was home to different groups of people at different times. Historians often divide it into two sections: Lower Nubia and Upper Nubia. Lower Nubia was to the north, closer to Egypt. Upper Nubia was to the south. Most of us think of "upper" as meaning north. But "upper" also means near the starting point of a river. Since the Nile flows from south to north, the upper Nile, and Upper Nubia, are to the south.

Scholars know more about Lower Nubia, the part closest to Egypt, in the early period of Nubian history. A famous archaeologist named George Reisner (RIZE-ner) excavated this area in the early 1900s. He found remains of ancient peoples he called the A-Group and the C-Group. (He also discovered people he called the B-Group, but these turned out to be a subgroup of the A-Group members, with fewer grave goods.) Because neither

Black Pharaohs from Nubia

Around 750 B.C., Egypt was in crisis. A number of different people claimed to be pharaoh. Some groups within Egypt supported one such man, a prince from Libya named Tefnakht (tef-NAKHT). Tefnakht conquered a number of Egyptian towns while trying to unify Egypt under his rule.

However, another man also claimed the Egyptian throne: the Nubian king Piye. He and his powerful army advanced north from Napata to Egypt and defeated Tefnakht. The Egyptians crowned Piye the first pharaoh of this black dynasty. Then Piye returned to his native Nubia and ruled Egypt from afar.

After Piye, his brother Shabako was crowned ruler of Egypt. Three more Nubian pharaohs followed. One of the Nubian pharaohs, Taharqa (ta-HAR-ka), was so proud to be crowned pharaoh of Egypt that he brought his mother over a thousand miles from Nubia to visit. After the ceremony he wrote how excited his mother was to see him upon the throne of Egypt.

The last Nubian pharaoh of Egypt was defeated by the Assyrians, who took over Egypt around 653 B.C. Nubian kings never again ruled Egypt. Instead, they brought many Egyptian customs to Nubia, where they continued to rule as pharaohs.

the A-Group nor the C-Group used writing, scholars know about them mostly from the things they left behind in their graves and other remains. It's too bad we don't know what these early people called themselves, so we could have more interesting names for them than letters of the alphabet!

The A-Group dressed in animal skins or leather, or else they wore nothing. They made necklaces and other jewelry from ostrich eggshells, seashells, or precious stones, or traded for finer jewelry from Egypt. They lived in tents or one-room houses made of stone or reeds. They buried their dead in shallow graves without coffins, placing food, drink, and sometimes ostrich-feather fans beside the bodies for the afterlife.

From very early times, the A-Group was in contact with Egypt. A-Group people were buried with many goods from Egypt: copper tools, linen cloth, and large jars that once held grain, wine, beer, or oil. (Some graves held so many rich objects that some scholars think they belonged to kings.) In exchange, the A-group Nubians must have sent the Egyptians trade goods from Nubia and farther south in Africa: ivory, ebony (a dark wood), perfumed oils, and ostrich eggs and feathers.

But Egypt wasn't satisfied with trade, especially once gold was discovered in Nubia. The Egyptian pharaohs began

Piye Loved Horses

King Piye's love of horses knew no earthly bounds. Following the war against Tefnakht, after which he was named pharaoh, he wrote how angry he was to see horses mistreated by Tefnakht. Piye had a team of horses buried near his tomb near Napata dressed in fine trappings. Four of his horses—his most valued possessions—were buried standing up, arranged as if they were pulling a chariot so that he could have them in the afterlife.

invading Nubia for the goods they craved. They built mines in the Nubian desert to dig beautiful hard stone for their monuments and later to mine for gold.

Scholars aren't sure why, but for about 600 years, between approximately 2900 and 2300 B.C., the original people of Lower Nubia seem to disappear. Perhaps they moved away because of the Egyptians' invasions or drought. After about 2300 B.C., the A-Group was no longer to be found.

Between about 2300 B.C. and about 1560 B.C. the C-Group lived in Lower Nubia. Their customs were much like the A-Group's, but they were cattle herders rather than farmers. They made fine pottery with carvings filled with various colors of paint. They placed ox skulls decorated with red and black dots near some of their graves and they continued burying people without coffins. Many took jobs as soldiers in the Egyptian army, traveling to distant lands to protect Egypt.

For a while Egypt pulled out of Nubia, during Egypt's First Intermediate Period. But during Egypt's Middle Kingdom, Egypt invaded again and controlled Lower Nubia between 2000 and 1750 B.C. The pharaohs were terrified of the Nubians, and built huge forts filled with soldiers around the Second Cataract on the Nile to control trade. Then Egypt entered its Second Intermediate Period, a time of political turmoil. Facing its own troubles at home, Egypt withdrew from Nubia again.

While Egypt occupied Lower Nubia, most Nubians steadfastly kept their own customs. But over time, especially after Egypt withdrew, some C-Group Nubians began to adopt Egyptian customs. Richer Nubians wore linen kilts like Egyptians' and adopted their burial customs. Not all Nubians adopted Egyptian ways. While many Nubians lived in rectangular Egyptian-style homes, others built traditional round houses like their ancestors, and continued Nubian burial styles.

Ancient Nubian Kingdoms

Little is certain about kingdoms in Lower Nubia. Some scholars feel the A-Group and C-Group Nubians lived in isolated villages; others disagree, saying the A-Group may have had kings. But in later years, three great kingdoms arose in Nubia. All began in Upper Nubia. All rose to their greatest power when Egypt was weak. One of these kingdoms even ruled Egypt for a time. These kingdoms were called Kerma, Napata, and Meroe (MARE-oh-way).

The first kingdom to arise was Kerma, in Upper Nubia, beginning about 2000 B.C. At first small, the kingdom grew most powerful when Egypt pulled back during its Second Intermediate Period. Kerma kings grew rich by ruling a large trading empire along the Nile, shipping fragrant woods, ivory, leopard skins, gold, and slaves north to Egypt. Several Kerma kings buried much of their wealth—including stone statues, weapons, and hundreds of living servants—in their huge, elaborate burial mounds.

Then, at the peak of Kerma's power, pharaohs of Egypt's New Kingdom invaded Nubia again. Around 1560 B.C. the city of Kerma was burned to the ground and its graveyard abandoned. The pharaohs claimed Upper and Lower Nubia as part of Egypt. They set up an Egyptian governor over the land, called the "King's Son of Kush." (This was just a title; he was not always the son of a king.) The Egyptians took Nubian princes as hostages to be raised with the sons of the pharaoh. The Nubian princes grew up learning Egyptian ways. Richer Nubians learned the Egyptian language and writing, and many followed Egyptian burial customs. Many Egyptians married Nubians and settled in Nubia.

For about 1,000 years, Egypt dominated Nubia. During this period, Egyptian

The God's Wives

Although Piye and his brothers were the real kings of Egypt, they lived far away in Nubia. Their daughters lived in Egypt, and each one acted on her father's behalf during his lifetime. While each woman ruled, her title was God's Wife of Amun, because she was thought to be married to the Egyptian god. A hieroglyphic text tells us about the festival that took place when one of these women, named Ankhnesneferibre (ANKE-nes-nefer-ib-re), became the new God's Wife. It says that when she went to the temple for her coronation, she was surrounded by Egyptian priests. She was specially dressed with amulets and crowned with a crown holding two tall plumes and a special golden diadem. She was then proclaimed the "queen of every circuit of the sun." The God's Wife was in charge of all of Egypt. When she died, she was buried on a bed underneath a tomb chapel in Luxor, in southern Egypt. The tombs include many Egyptian-style objects, like *ushabtis* (servant statues) and stone jars to hold internal organs.

pharaohs built many monuments and temples in Nubia. Ramses II completed a temple beside a sacred mountain, now called Gebel Barkal (JEB-bell BAR-kal). Part of this mountain was shaped like a *uraeus* (you-RAY-us), the cobra symbol of Egypt that pharaohs wore on their brows. Ramses dedicated the temple to the Egyptian god Amun, king of heaven. Under Egyptian rule, the worship of Amun and other Egyptian gods and goddesses spread across Upper and Lower Nubia. The Egyptians withdrew from Nubia around 1070 B.C. when turmoil arose in their own land.

The next famous Nubian kingdom arose a hundred or more years later—scholars are not sure exactly when. It began in Napata, a town in Upper Nubia near the sacred mountain Gebel Barkal. One of the Napatan kings, Piye (Pee-YAY), restored the temple built by the Egyptians to Amun. Nubian priests worshipped Amun within the temple. Amun was shown as a man with the head of a ram. Later Napatan kings and queens were crowned there. Piye accomplished what no other Nubian king before him had done—he became the first Nubian king to rule Egypt as well as Nubia, beginning about 747 B.C.

Hundreds of years later, the kings of Napata moved their capital south, to a town called Meroe where more rain fell. In Meroe, Nubian culture truly flourished. The people of Meroe developed new kinds of arts and crafts. They made tools from iron and painted pottery with vivid animals and plants. They invented their own alphabet. Instead of writing in Egyptian, they wrote in their own language, called Meroitic (mare-oh-IT-ik).

Meroitic queens and kings were both honored, and the country was sometimes ruled by a queen. Queen Shanakdakhete (sha-nak-da-KHE-te) ruled from about 170 to 150 B.C. She seems to have ruled without a king. The mother of the king was also a person of importance, with her own title—Kandake (kan-DA-ke). (Ancient historians from Greece and Rome wrote that a Nubian queen named Candace fought against the Roman Emperor Augustus. They were probably confused by the title Kandake and thought it was a name.)

The Nubians in Meroe traded with both the Romans and the Greeks. When the Romans conquered Egypt in 30 B.C., they did not succeed in conquering Nubia. Nubia was a powerful and independent kingdom well into the next millennium.

Nubian Architecture

Buildings in ancient Nubia ranged from the humble to the spectacular and included palaces, temples, meeting places, and homes. Some of the most spectacular buildings, like the massive temple at Abu Simbel, were built by Egyptian pharaohs.

In Kerma, two huge artificial mountains made by the Nubians from clay brick loomed over the city. The Nubians considered them homes of the gods.

But most buildings were very simple. At different times and places, people lived in houses built of straw, wood, rocks, or mud brick. Many were designed like Egyptian houses, with rectangular rooms made of mud brick and flat roofs. But throughout the history of Nubia, some people lived in one-room circular houses called *tukls* (TOO-kls). Even in our own century, some Nubians live in these traditional round homes.

In the ancient village of Aniba, houses were made by standing big slabs of stone in a circle, with smaller rocks or branches on top. The roof was probably thatch held up by wooden poles. An entryway of clay bricks kept people from seeing within. Inside, the Nubians built fires in pits lined with stones.

Imaginary Nubian House

What would it be like for you and your family to live in a round, one-room house?

Materials

▲ *Bowl or saucer about 6 inches across, for tracing around*
▲ *Paper*
▲ *Pencil*

Directions

Draw a circle on your paper by tracing around the bowl or saucer. Imagine that this circle is a house that you are looking down on from above. Draw a doorway.

Now imagine what it would be like to live here for years. What would you and your family need? Draw pictures of the inside of the house. Put in

view from above

anything you think you would want for eating, sleeping, storage, working, or fun. If you like, you can pretend you have electricity, plumbing, and phone service. Or you can pretend you are in ancient Nubia, and have only the things ancient Nubians would have.

Now imagine that you are sharing this house with two other families. What would you keep? What wouldn't there be room for? If you like, draw another picture.

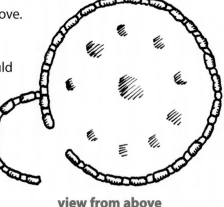

Houses like these were built by northern Nubians before the Napatan Period in a town called Aniba. The lower part was built of stone slabs placed on end. Wood beams supported the roof. A curving entrance kept people outside from seeing in. *Courtesy of J. J. Augustin, Glückstadt, artist renditions*

Model Mud-Brick House

You can make a miniature *tukl*, or circular house, like the ones early Nubians lived in.

Materials

- ▲ 1 piece heavy cardboard at least 9 by 5 inches square
- ▲ Aluminum foil
- ▲ Tape
- ▲ Lid or saucer for tracing, 3 or 4 inches across
- ▲ Pen
- ▲ Self-hardening clay such as Marblex, or ordinary potter's clay
- ▲ Clay tools or pencil
- ▲ 4 straight twigs 2 or 3 inches long (or pipe cleaners folded to the right length)
- ▲ Lid or saucer for tracing, 5 or 6 inches across
- ▲ 1 sheet brown construction paper
- ▲ Scissors
- ▲ Small piece yellow construction paper (optional)

Directions

Cover the cardboard with aluminum foil to use as a base for the model. Tape the foil down on the back of the cardboard.

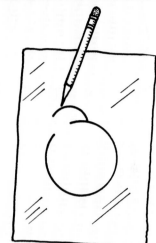

Trace around the smaller lid onto your covered cardboard. This is the outline for your tukl. Add a curved line attached to the circle for an entryway.

Roll a ball of clay and press it flat into the middle of your circle. Completely fill in the circle with thick clay. This will be the floor.

Make a wall around the circle with more flattened clay. Before you put up the wall, dig lines into it with an old pencil to suggest rocks. Seal the wall to the edge of the floor, leaving an opening for the door. Flatten clay for the entryway wall. You can scratch lines on this piece of clay to

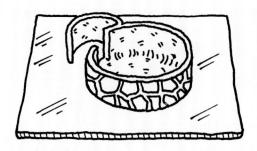

look like bricks. Stand the piece of clay along the line you drew for the entry. Make a dent in the middle of the floor for a fire-place. Cut a small piece of yellow construction paper for flames and stick it into the clay.

Stand the two tallest twigs near the middle of the tukl. Stand a couple of shorter twigs near the edge, closer to the walls. The twigs will hold up the roof. The smaller twigs should be slightly taller than the walls.

To make the roof, trace around the larger lid onto brown paper. Cut out the circle. Draw a dot in the center of the circle. You will be shaping this circle into a cone.

Twigs should be slightly taller than the walls.

Draw two dots on the edge of the circle right next to each other. Draw a straight line from each dot on the edge to the center of the circle. The lines should touch each other as they come closer to the center. This shape should look like a thin pie slice. Cut along the two lines all the way to the center of the circle. Discard the pie-shaped piece you cut out. Hold the circle in two hands and push the two lines you cut toward each other until one side slides slightly under the other. This makes the cone. Before taping the cone, hold it over the top of the tukl. Make sure the bottom of the cone is a little wider than the circular walls.

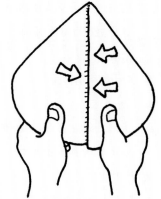

Tape the cone on the inside and the outside.

Put the roof in place.

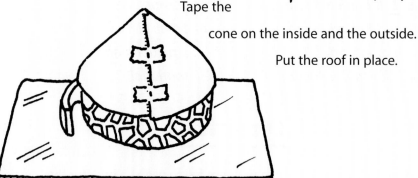

Nubian Clothing

Most of the garments of early Nubians were made of leather from the skins of cattle, sheep, and goats. At other times Nubians tied leopard or gazelle skins into kilts. Sometimes they wore leather sandals and caps, and belts made of woven linen or leather. Men, women, and children wore jewelry, including necklaces, bracelets, arm bands, earrings, and rings. Men and women wore makeup around their eyes. We're not sure why they did this; perhaps it was to prevent eye disease, deflect the sun, or for religious purposes. Or perhaps, like many peoples, they found the eye makeup beautiful. Sometimes they wore tall ostrich feathers in their hair.

Nubians decorated their clothing. They stamped designs onto leather or dyed it red. In Kerma, some wore leather clothing decorated with beads in fancy patterns or designs made of punched holes.

Many Nubians wore tattoos and purposely scarred their faces in different patterns. No one is certain exactly why they did this, but tattooing is a favorite body ornament in many world cultures. Hairstyles varied. Sometimes men or women wore many tiny braids. Other times they cut their hair short. Women from the C-Group often wore hair clips made of shell.

Fashions changed over time, and rich people often dressed differently from the poor. For example, some Kerman men wore only goatskins tied around their waists, and leather sandals. Others added linen robes, beaded belts, or caps with feathers. Many servants buried in Kerman kings' tombs wore caps stitched with tiny animals carved of glittery mica. At different times in Nubian history, Nubians who had lived in Egypt or in close contact with Egyptians adopted Egyptian fashions. Women wore linen dresses and colored collars. Men wore pleated linen kilts. They might combine these with traditional Nubian ostrich feathers and heavy round earrings.

Kings and queens in Napata and Meroe developed their own blend of Nubian and Egyptian styles. They wore red fringed shawls over long linen gowns with colored borders. Kings and queens wore a lot of gold jewelry, including necklaces, collars, bracelets on their wrists and upper arms, and anklets (bracelets for the ankles).

This image of King Arnekhamani (235–218 B.C.) of Meroe is carved on a wall of the Lion Temple at Musawwarat-es-Sufra. Notice the king's elaborate fringed shawl, his close-fitting cap, the cobra over his forehead, and the streamers down the back of his neck. He wears a special guard on his right thumb to protect it while shooting arrows. *Courtesy of Humboldt Universität, Berlin and Brooklyn Museum of Art*

Napatan and Meroitic kings or queens wore a special headdress (a small skullcap covered the top of the head). A ribbon trailed down the back of the neck. Two cobras made of gold leaned out from the ruler's forehead.

Egyptian pharaohs wore a similar cobra, called a *uraeus* (you-RAY-us), on their heads, but usually only one. The uraeus stood for kingship. In Nubia the rulers wore two golden cobras side by side. The two cobras may have reminded them of the glorious days when Nubia's kings ruled both Egypt and Nubia.

Royal Headdress

You can make a headdress with a double cobra similiar to the ones ancient Nubian royalty wore.

Materials

▲ *1 piece cloth or ribbon, 1 to 2 inches wide and long enough to tie around your head with an extra 15–20 inches*

▲ *2 long pipe cleaners, gold if possible. If they are white, color them gold or yellow.*

Directions

Make sure the ribbon is long enough by tying it around your head. It should cross your forehead low over your eyebrows. Knot it behind your head with the ends trailing down your neck.

Make a cobra, or uraeus.

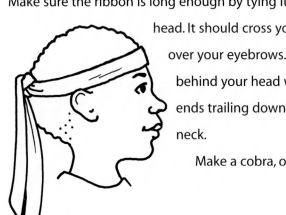

Fold one pipe cleaner in half. The folded tip will be the head of the cobra. Bend the pipe cleaner into the shape of a cobra raising its head. Leave at least 2 inches for the tail. Make another cobra from the second pipe cleaner. Take off the ribbon and fold it in two to find the middle. Unfold it, marking the middle with an object or a pencil mark. Put the two cobras side by side at the middle of the ribbon. Hook their tails underneath and behind the ribbon, then over the top. The pointy ends should end up facing front, where they won't stick you.

Tie the ribbon around your head, with the cobras jutting forward from the middle of your forehead.

Royal Robe

You can dress like a Nubian king or queen from Napata or Meroe. Here are two ways to make this robe, the first using a piece of cloth and the second using an old shirt.

Method One
Materials

- ▲ 1 large piece plain white or colored cloth, at least 36 inches wide. It should be twice the length of your body from your shoulders to your ankles. An old sheet works well.
- ▲ Pencil or pen
- ▲ Wide-tipped markers in several colors
- ▲ Scissors
- ▲ Safety pins or masking tape

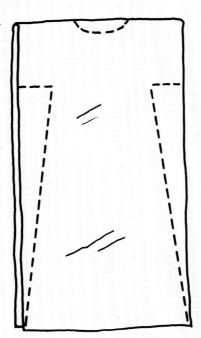

Directions

Lay the cloth out on a table or floor. Fold it in half the long way. Copy the pattern in the picture shown here directly onto the fabric with a pencil or pen. Make sure you've drawn the pattern wide enough so you can fit inside it with a couple of inches on either side. Make sure the sleeves are extra wide, too.

Cut along the lines you drew.

Fasten the sides with safety pins or tape. Turn the robe inside out.

Decorate the collar, hem, and ends of the sleeves with markers. Copy the patterns shown on this dress or design your own.

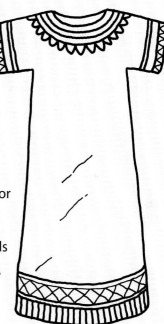

Method Two
Materials

- ▲ 1 old short-sleeved T-shirt that no one needs anymore. It should come down to your knees. A light, solid color is best. (Hint: if there's a pattern on the front, turn it inside out with the pattern in back.)
- ▲ Wide-tipped markers in several colors

Directions

Decorate the collar, hem, and ends of the sleeves with markers. Copy the patterns shown on the previous page or design your own.

Earrings

It's easy to make impressive earrings like the ones many Nubians wore.

Materials

- ▲ Gold pipe cleaner
- ▲ Scissors

Directions

Cut the gold pipe cleaner in two. Set aside one half. Fold one of the pieces in two. Bend it into a circle with the ends nearly touching. Hook it onto the lower part of your ear.

Do the same with the other piece of pipe cleaner.

Now, put on your headdress, robe, shawl (see next activity), and earrings. If you like, put on sandals or extra jewelry. Compare yourself to the picture of King Arnekhamani. How closely do you match this royal image?

Fringed Shawl

Ancient Napatan and Meroitic kings and queens wore special red fringed shawls. If you've made all the Nubian clothing, you can wear it together and look like royalty.

Materials

▲ *1 strip old cloth, 6 to 10 inches wide and at least 1 yard long. Red is best.*
▲ *Scissors*
▲ *Safety pin*
▲ *Markers (optional)*

Directions

Cut fringes along one long side of the cloth. The fringes should be three or four inches long.

Decorate the nonfringed area with markers. You can draw circles, diamonds, or stripes.

Drape the shawl over your right shoulder and across your front (like the picture on page 108). Fasten the ends together with the pin.

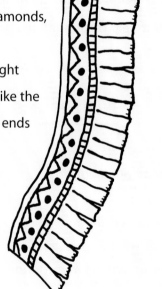

Nubian Hair Clip

This hair clip is based on ones that women and men wore in northern Nubia before the days of the Kerma Kingdom (before 2000 B.C.). Nubians carved these clips out of shell. Instead of using shell, you carve a hair clip from a Styrofoam meat tray. Ask for a clean one at the meat counter in the supermarket.

Adult help recommended with the craft knife.

Materials

▲ Newspapers
▲ Styrofoam meat tray
▲ Scissors
▲ Pen or pencil
▲ Craft knife
▲ Permanent markers (optional)

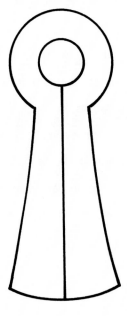

Directions

Put the pile of newspapers on your work surface to protect it before you use the craft knife. With the scissors, cut a flat piece of Styrofoam from the meat tray, about three inches square. Copy the illustration on this page onto the Styrofoam you cut, about the same size as the picture. Cut out the outline with the craft knife. Make a single cut to separate the two "legs." Cut out the inner round shape. Don't worry if it's a little ragged—it will stay in your hair better.

If you use a white meat tray, you can color it with permanent markers. Try a blend of yellow, pink, and orange to make the color of a shell.

Wear your clip in your hair. If it slides out, try wearing it on the side of your head with your hair pulled back in a ponytail. You can also wear it on a ribbon around your neck. If people ask you about it, you can say it's a prehistoric bobby pin.

Nubian Writing

Writing was invented in Mesopotamia. The idea spread to Egypt and inspired hieroglyphic script. It took many centuries for other people to learn about reading and writing. When they did, they usually borrowed the writing system they saw. The Hittites borrowed Mesopotamian cuneiform. The Nubians used Egyptian hieroglyphs.

About 100 B.C. the Nubians began to use their own writing system. The Nubian script is called *Meroitic*, after Meroe, where it was first used. It is made up of 23 signs and could be written in two different ways. One form, called *hieroglyphic*, was very similar to Egyptian hieroglyphs. This form was used for carving in stone on tombs or temple walls. Most of these carvings were commanded by the king or queen.

The other form, usually called *cursive*, was written on papyrus, animal skins, and on stone. Most Meroitic writing used this form. Eventually it replaced Meroitic hieroglyphs on most public buildings and tombs.

The Meroitic alphabet was based on the Egyptian hieroglyphic alphabet. Many of the letters and the sounds they stand for are the same. But other symbols stand for different sounds. And some Meroitic symbols are brand new. They may stand for sounds in the Nubian language that are different from sounds in Egyptian. Some symbols stand for sounds that don't exist in English.

Like the Egyptians, the Nubians sometimes wrote from top to bottom, often from right to left, and sometimes from left to right. The letters faced the beginning of the line.

Unlike the Egyptians, the Nubians used dots to show where one word ended and another began. Sometimes they used two dots and sometimes three.

An Ancient Inscription

An actual cursive Meroitic inscription (on the top of the next page), one that appears often on tombs, means, "O Isis, O Osiris," calling on two Egyptian gods. Osiris was lord of the underworld. Isis was both his sister and his wife. Meroitic people pronounced the names differently from the Egyptians. They called Isis *Wosh*. Instead of saying "O" in front of each name, they put an *i* at the end. They wrote "Woshi" instead of "O Wosh." In this inscription, they wrote from right to left.

Look at the cursive Meroitic alphabet. Can you figure out which word in the inscription stands for "O Isis?" How do you think the Nubians pronounced "O Osiris?" The people of Meroe used their own alphabet, although they adopted many characters from Egyptian hieroglyphic. Most Meroitic writing used the form called "cursive." *Adapted alphabet courtesy of Humboldt Universität, Berlin and Brooklyn Museum of Art*

Hieroglyphic	Cursive	English Translation	Hieroglyphic	Cursive	English Translation
		a			L
		e			h
		i			h (underlined)
		o			sh
		y			s (se)
		w			k
		b			q
		p			t
		m			te
		n			to
		ñ (ne) (nye)			d
		r			word divider

Reading and Writing Using the Meroitic Alphabet

Many people today are learning to write in Egyptian hiero-glyphs. But very few people can use the Meroitic alphabet. Here's a way to create truly secret messages.

Nubian Reading

In the following sentence, substitute English letters for the Meroitic ones and see what the message says. Note: the symbol is used for the sound "u" since there is no "u" in Meroitic.

Nubian Writing

Try writing a few words in English using Meroitic hieroglyphs. If letters you need are missing, use letters for similar sounds. If you can't find a sound close enough, write the letter in English, or make up your own symbol.

Scholars learned what Meroitic letters sounded like by reading names of kings or gods. These names were sometimes written in both Egyptian and Meroitic. Since the scholars knew how to pronounce the names in Egyptian, they could figure out how to pronounce the Meroitic letters.

The Meroitic alphabet is not hard to read, compared to other writing systems like cuneiform. But scholars have immense diffi-culty interpreting Meroitic writings. Why? Because no one today speaks Meroitic or any language close to it, and because there are not many inscriptions to study, we know the meanings of only a few Meroitic words.

This is an actual tomb inscription. It translates as "O Isis, O Isiris."

This translates as "Peter Peter pumpkin eater."

118

Nubian Work

Most Nubians farmed and herded animals. They also wove cloth and baskets, tanned leather, carved wood, hunted, fished, and cooked. They made clay pots by hand, some of them so delicate they look as if they were made on a potter's wheel. In later times, they used a potter's wheel as well as continuing to make hand-built pots.

The Nubians made many of the things they used every day. Most people did these things for their own families. Some people traded their work with others.

Other Nubians worked as scribes, soldiers, priests or priestesses of Amun or other gods, or as servants or guards. There were no schools that we know of. Children learned by doing.

Model Irrigation Machine

Farming involved many tasks: plowing the land, sowing the seed, bringing water to the crops, and harvesting. Without rain, Nubians farmed the land that was flooded by the Nile. But in much of Nubia, this strip of land was narrow. Nubians, like Egyptians and other ancient peoples, irrigated some of their fields. Irrigation let them grow crops on a bit more land.

The earliest Nubians used simple methods to irrigate. They lowered empty buckets into the Nile and raised them up full of water. They dumped the water into ditches they'd dug to other fields, or poured it around the bases of trees. This was hard work and had to be repeated over and over.

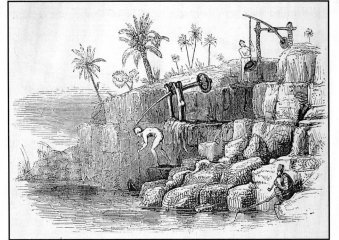

In this 150-year-old picture, Egyptians are using shadufs to draw water. The shaduf was imported into Egypt and Nubia from Mesopotamia thousands of years ago. Shadufs are still used in many villages in Africa and southern Asia. *Courtesy of Sir J. Gardner Wilkinson,* A Popular Account of the Ancient Egyptians, *Library of Congress*

Sometime in their history, the Nubians learned about an invention that is still used today in Egypt, the Sudan, and other parts of Africa. It is usually called by an Arabic name, *shaduf* (sha-DOOF). With a shaduf, Nubians could lift full buckets more easily.

How did a shaduf work? It was similar to a seesaw in its design. A wooden arm rested across an upright base. A weight made of mud was fitted to one end. The bucket hung from the other end, tied onto a rope or wooden handle. The base could be made in different ways. Some shadufs had bases made from branches, mud, or reeds bundled together. Others had bases made by laying a piece of wood across two upright forked posts.

With a shaduf, the Nubians could lower a bucket into the water and then pull up on the rope to make the full bucket rise. The weight at the back of the shaduf helped raise the heavy bucket. Once the bucket was high enough so that it could be grabbed by hand, they poured the water into a nearby ditch. The ditch carried the water to the thirsty plants.

You can make a model shaduf that actually works! Instead of a clay bucket, you'll use a thimble. This craft is complicated. Plan to take two hours.

Adult help recommended with the pocket knife.

Materials

- ▲ 6-inch-long dowel, $1/2$ inch in diameter
- ▲ Tape measure
- ▲ Pencil or pen
- ▲ Pocket knife
- ▲ Roll of twine
- ▲ Scissors
- ▲ 2 strong forked sticks, about 7 inches tall from base to fork and $1/2$ inch across the bottom; forks should be 1 to 2 inches long
- ▲ 1 16-inch-long dowel, $3/4$ inch in diameter
- ▲ 5 pennies
- ▲ Duct tape

- ▲ Thimble
- ▲ 1 sheet aluminum foil, at least 12 by 16 inches (extra-strong is best)
- ▲ Disposable aluminum baking pan, approximately 2 inches deep and 13 by 9 inches around
- ▲ 8 cups dirt, well packed
- ▲ Trowel
- ▲ 1 sheet aluminum foil, about 2 inches by 8 inches
- ▲ Cup
- ▲ Water

Directions

Making the Shaduf

Measure the six-inch-long dowel and mark the middle. With the knife, cut a shallow notch at the spot you marked. Cut the notch all the way around the dowel. Get an adult to help you with this.

Cut a piece of twine about two feet long. Tie one end tightly around one of the forked sticks, just below the fork. Do the same with the other stick, using another piece of twine.

Lay the short dowel across the two forks. Have someone stand the sticks upright while you tie the short dowel snugly in place. You have now made the stand for the shaduf.

Begin the next part of the shaduf, the pole that holds the weight and the bucket. Measure the 16-inch-long dowel and mark a spot $9^1/2$ inches from one end. Cut a shallow notch all the way around the dowel at this spot.

Stack the pennies. Using duct tape, fasten them to the end of the dowel nearest the notch.

Cut a 12-inch length of twine to hold the bucket. Tie one end tightly around the other end of the dowel. Wrap a small piece of duct tape around the knot.

Cut a two-inch length of twine for a handle for the bucket (thimble). Cut a piece of duct tape to wrap around the bucket and fasten the twine to the bucket with the duct tape. Use a square knot to tie the bucket handle to the twine at the end of the pole.

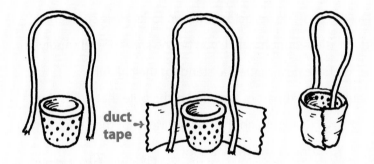

duct → tape

Cut another piece of twine three feet long. Use it to tie the long dowel to the stand. It must be tied tightly around each dowel, but loose enough in between so the long dowel can rock back and forth.

square knot

Here's how:

1. First tie the twine snugly around the notched part in the long dowel, using a square knot. Leave a tail. Wrap the twine tightly several times around the long dowel near the notch.

2. Leaving a little slack, bring the twine around the notched part of the stand. Wrap it snugly several times within the notch.

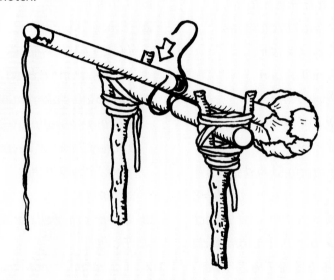

3. Make a somewhat loose figure-eight with the twine. Wrap it over the long dowel, then under the short dowel on one side, then back over the long dowel, then under the short dowel on the opposite side. Repeat several times. Keep the twine somewhat loose. When you're near the end of the twine, knot it to the tail you left.

Making Part of the Nile

Lay a piece of aluminum foil in front of you with one of the long sides nearest you. Draw a line across the foil 4 inches from the edge nearest you. Fold the edge so it stands straight up. Place the aluminum foil across one end of the baking pan. Position it the long way, so most of the excess foil laps over the two sides of the pan. The foil should cover about ⅓ of the pan, with the folded part nearest the middle of the pan. Now carefully, without tearing, line the end of the pan with the foil. Push the foil to the bottom of the pan, leaving the folded part upright so it forms a wall. Wrap the other edges of the foil over the sides and end of the pan. You are making an area that will hold water, so start over with a new piece of foil if you make a hole.

Using the trowel, scoop the dirt into the part of the pan that is not lined with foil. Pack it in so it comes up to the top of the pan.

Make a crease level with the top of the dirt in the upright piece of foil. Fold it back so it covers the edge of the dirt. Now

hide that part of the foil by covering it with a thin layer of dirt.

Stick the shaduf into the dirt farthest from the water. Pack dirt securely around the legs. If it tips, your dirt may be too light. To fix, you can add a bit of water and mix it in with the dirt, or use

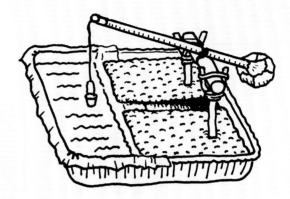

heavier dirt. Make an irrigation ditch from just behind the riverbank to the back of the baking pan. Try to make the rear of the ditch deeper than the part nearest the river. Line it with the extra piece of aluminum foil. Use a cup to pour water into the Nile.

Test your shaduf. Pull gently on the string holding the bucket to lower the bucket into the water. Now pull up on the string to raise the bucket. With your fingers, move the bucket and empty it into the drainage ditch. (Although it's fun to manipulate the model shaduf using the back of the pole, ancient people did not do that.)

(Note: Some thimbles are heavier than others. You may need to add more pennies to balance your shaduf.)

Nubian Food

Nubians had a limited diet because their land was so harsh. Still, they raised and ate many foods in common with the Egyptians, Mesopotamians, and Hittites. They ate grains, dates, figs, and nuts, and drank milk. On special occasions, they ate meat from cattle, sheep, and goats. Sometimes, ancient Nubians ate more exotic meats such as hippopotamus, ostrich, turtle, and gazelle.

The Nubians usually harvested wheat and barley in the winter. In the summer they gathered a wild grain called *sorghum* (SORE-gum). Like modern Nubians, they may have made sorghum into a kind of porridge or baked it into flat loaves like pancakes.

They also grew a grain called *millet*. Millet looks like tiny yellow balls. It's a common ingredient in hamster food and birdseed. People who are allergic to wheat can use millet flour to bake bread.

The Nile attracted water birds like ducks and geese, so Nubians added these to their diet, as well as fish like Nile perch and mudfish. Sometimes they made the fish into sauce. Fish was not always considered an acceptable food, maybe for religious reasons.

One of King Piye's inscriptions described some people as "eaters of fish, which is an abomination to the House of the King."

Nubians drank beer, wine, and milk. They made beer from barley. Grapes needed for wine didn't grow well, although the Nubians did have vineyards. The Nubians imported most of their wine from Egypt. They also imported Egyptian cooking oil, honey, and cheese. The clay jars that stored these foods have been found in many ancient Nubian ruins.

Nubians probably also grew and ate lentils, beans, onions, and green vegetables such as lettuce.

During hard times, most Nubians survived on little food. But in Meroe, royalty ate well. The Meroitic queens and princesses in pictures were plump!

Millet Breakfast Porridge

This recipe uses ancient Nubian ingredients. You can find millet in most natural food stores.

Adult help recommended with the stove.

2 servings

Ingredients

▲ *1 cup water*
▲ *Pinch salt*
▲ *¼ cup millet*
▲ *2 dates*

▲ *2 tablespoons broken nut pieces (not peanuts)*
▲ *½ cup milk*

Utensils

▲ *Measuring cup*
▲ *Pot with tight-fitting lid*
▲ *Stove*
▲ *Large spoon*
▲ *Timer*

▲ *Cutting board or plate*
▲ *Plastic knife*
▲ *Measuring spoon*
▲ *Serving bowls*

Directions

Put the water into the pot, place it on stove, and turn the heat to high. Add the salt.

When the water boils, add the millet and stir briefly. Turn down the heat to low, cover the pot, and set the timer to 25 minutes.

Remove the pits from the dates. Chop the dates with the knife and add the dates and nuts to the pot. Cover the pot.

Stir the millet occasionally to make sure the grain doesn't stick and burn.

After the 25 minutes are up, turn off the heat and spoon the millet into bowls.

Pour a little milk on top of each serving.

Nubian Religion

M ost of what we know about Nubian religion comes from burials, ruined temples, and inscriptions on temple walls. Ancient Nubians placed food and drink around their dead to help them in the afterlife. They worshipped gods, many of them borrowed from the Egyptians. Their most important god was Amun. Amun, an Egyptian god, was often shown in pictures with a head like a sheep. Nubians during the Napatan Kingdom (beginning around 900 B.C.) built Egyptian-style temples to these gods.

Nubian royal pyramids were smaller and steeper than the early pyramids from Egypt. This drawing of the pyramid of Queen Amanishakheto of Meroe was made more than 150 years ago. Many Nubian pyramids, including King Piye's, no longer stand. *Courtesy of Frédéric Cailliaud,* Voyage à Meroé, *Library of Congress*

During the Meroitic period, Nubians also built temples to Apedemak, a god with the head of a lion. One inscription to Apedemak says:

You are greeted, Apedemak . . . great god . . . lion of the south, strong of arm. . . . The one who carries the secret, concealed in his being. . . . Who is a companion for men and women . . . the one who hurls his hot breath against his enemy. You are called "Great of Power." . . . The one who punishes all who commit crimes against him. . . . Who gives to those who call to him. . . . Lord of life . . .

—translated by Professor P. L. Shinnie

The Lion-God: Making a Myth

You can make up a myth about a Nubian god. *Myths* are ways of telling stories about the gods: where they came from, what they did, what they were like. We know less about Apedemak than we do about Egyptian gods.

Directions

Make up a myth about Apedemak. Fill in some of the gaps in our knowledge. How was he created? Did he have brothers and sisters? Were they also gods? How did he come to be a god?

Nubians in the Meroitic Kingdom worshipped the lion-god Apedemak. Although other gods and goddesses were adopted from the Egyptians, Apedemak was originally Meroitic. Later pictures sometimes show him with wings or the body of a snake. *Courtesy of Walters Art Gallery, Baltimore*

Burials

Early Nubians were not mummified. They were buried in the sand in pits, sometimes covered by mounds, along with a few goods for the afterlife such as pottery jars of food, personal ornaments, and arrowheads. In Kerma, the burials of kings grew more and more elaborate as the kingdom grew rich. The king's tomb was covered with a mound of sand and earth the size of a city block. Gold, ivory, and other riches were heaped inside the tomb. Sheep—sometimes wearing elaborate headdresses of ostrich plumes—were buried with them. So were human servants. In one tomb, more than 300 men, women, and children—dressed in their finest clothing—were buried alive alongside their king when he died.

When the Nubian king Piye became ruler of Egypt, he brought Egyptian customs back to Nubia. He ruled both Egypt and Nubia from his home in Napata. Many scholars believe he was the first Nubian to build a pyramid. Later kings and queens from Napata and Meroe were all buried under pyramids.

Nubian pyramids had steeper sides and were much smaller than the famous pyramids in Egypt. The tops of the pyramids were flat, not pointed, sometimes with a little pillar on top designed like a flower. The sides were built of good-quality stone. Inside, the pyramid was filled with rubble. The body wasn't actually inside the pyramid. It was in a chamber carved out of the rock underneath.

In the floor of the burial chamber was a raised platform to hold the coffin or body. As in Kerma, sometimes the king's body was placed on a bed instead of in a coffin. Inside Piye's burial chamber was an Egyptian-style stone bench and a coffin. In a combination of Egyptian and Nubian custom, he may have had his coffin placed on a bed that stood on the bench.

The First Nubian Pyramid: Piye's Tomb

When Piye died, he may not have been mummified. There were stone jars in Piye's tomb to contain his internal organs, just as in burials of Egyptian mummies. But the jars were fakes. Underneath the lids, the jars were solid stone.

Later royal Nubians were mummified. But the custom never spread to common people. Natron, the mineral used in mummification, did not occur naturally in Nubia but had to be shipped from Egypt. It was too expensive for ordinary people to use.

You can make a model of the first pyramid ever built in Nubia.

Materials

▲ 2 pounds clay—either self-hardening clay such as Marblex, or ordinary potter's clay
▲ Damp rag to cover clay
▲ 1 piece heavy cardboard 9 inches square, covered with aluminum foil, or a heavy paper plate
▲ Plastic knife
▲ Old pencil

▲ 1 piece medium cardboard (from the back of a notepad)
▲ Scissors
▲ Scrap paper (an old paper lunch bag works well)

Directions

Take a lump of clay about the size of your fist and knead it firmly. Repeat this until you have kneaded all the clay. Put about one-fourth of the clay aside and cover it with the damp rag. Work the rest of the clay into a square about 1½ inches thick and 3 or 4 inches long on each side. Put it on the paper plate or foil-covered cardboard.

First you will dig out the tomb chamber. Then you will build a staircase leading down into the tomb chamber from the top of the clay. Finally, you will use your extra clay to build a pyramid over the tomb. The pyramid will stand on a removable cardboard base so you can lift it off and see inside.

To make the tomb chamber, dig a square hole about two inches wide near one end of the clay block. Make sure your hole doesn't go all the way through the bottom. The

3–4 inches   3–4 inches

1½ inches

hole will be the tomb chamber. Smooth the walls but keep the hole square.

Now begin the staircase. Choose the side closest to the middle of the block. Start at the bottom of that side and take away clay to make a slope. Your slope should reach the top near the end of the clay block. Use your pencil to cut steps in the slope. You can make stripes to look like steps.

Smooth the floor of the burial chamber. If you like, use a small extra piece of clay to make a bench for the coffin. You can also make some tiny jars or other objects to put in the tomb.

Cut a square piece of medium cardboard a little bigger than the top of the hole. This will be a removable cover for the tomb. (In real life, of course, this wasn't removable—it was solid brick or rock.) Lay the cover on top of the hole.

Use the clay you set aside to begin the pyramid on top of the cover. Roll a skinny snake shape with some of the clay and cut it into four

equal pieces. Lay the pieces on the square cover, right next to the edge, to form a square.

Now make another snake and cut it in four. Make each piece a little shorter than the previous pieces. Lay the pieces on top of the first row, but slightly closer to the center of the square. This will make the sides angle in, as a pyramid does. Repeat this procedure three more times to form the lower part of your pyramid.

Before your pyramid gets too high, make some rubble. Rip the scrap paper into pieces and roll them into little balls. Fill the middle of the pyramid with these "rocks." Make more snakes and build up the four sides of the pyramid until they come together at the top. Add more rubble just before you bring the four sides together. Leave the top of the pyramid flat and smooth it over the rubble. Smooth the sides of the pyramid. Use the pencil to scratch lines that look like big stones on the outside.

Use your pencil to scratch "Piye's Tomb" on the base.

Conclusion

For years, many scholars viewed Nubia as a group of minor cultures, important only because of their relations with Egypt. They didn't recognize that Nubia had an exciting heritage of its own. Archaeologists have discovered much about the ancient kingdoms and cultures of Nubia. But mysteries remain.

Where was the ancient city of Napata? When, precisely, did it first emerge? What are the meanings of Meroitic inscriptions? We can pronounce the letters, but the sounds are meaningless because no one knows the language being written. How did the kingdom of Meroe ward off the Romans, who defeated mighty Egypt and much of Europe? So many questions still await researchers—these and more.

Kings and queens, farmers and herders, glittering cities and humble stone huts lie buried in the Nubian sands, their stories untold. The answers to our questions lie buried with them—perhaps to be unearthed in time.

The Hittites

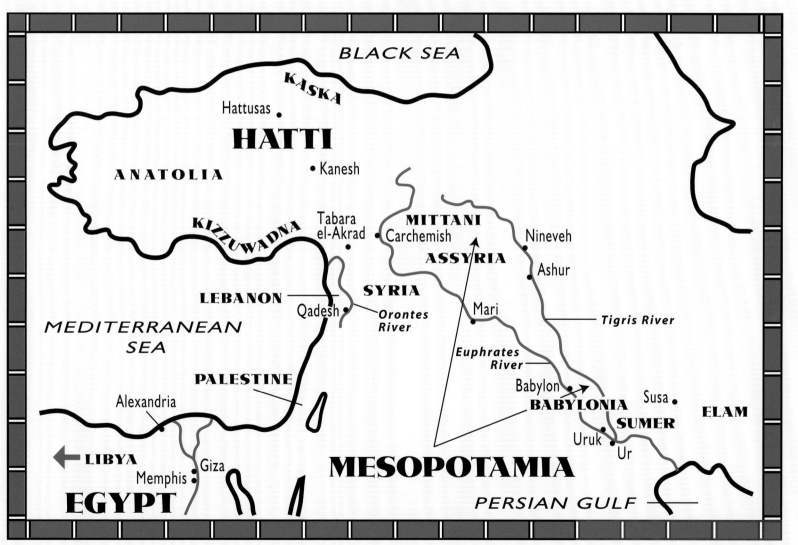

Hittite History and Geography

For thousands of years, crumbling walls of gray stone dotted a windswept hillside in northern Turkey. The local people didn't know who had left these ruins. In 1834, less than two centuries ago, a traveling Frenchman was impressed by the weathered stone walls. He believed they might once have been part of a great city, but he couldn't determine who had built it or who lived in this city. The Frenchman published pictures of the ruins throughout Europe to discover if someone else could identify these ruins. Among all the theories that people proposed, no one suggested that it might have belonged to the Hittites.

Before the 1800s, few people thought of the Hittites at all. Although they were mentioned in the Bible, scholars believed the Hittites were only a small tribe living far southeast of Turkey, perhaps in Canaan (modern-day Israel). Then archaeologists discovered documents in Egypt mentioning the Hittites. One document was a peace treaty between Pharaoh Ramses II and the Hittite king Hattusilis III, carved in hieroglyphs on an Egyptian temple wall.

Would Ramses II have bothered to write such a treaty with the chief of a minor tribe? It didn't seem likely. Scholars began to believe the Hittites might have been a powerful culture based in Syria. Why Syria? A few mysterious inscriptions were found there that some claimed were Hittite remains. Some scholars proposed that the Hittite center of power was in Syria, with outposts in other countries such as Turkey. Then a discovery astonished the world.

In 1906, a German scholar named Hugo Winckler went to Turkey to study the ruined city on the hill. He had heard that carvings had been found there that matched the strange inscriptions found in Syria. He believed these inscriptions were Hittite. Perhaps, he thought, the ruins in Turkey might be a Hittite settlement. Professor Winckler hired local workmen to dig in the Turkish ruins. Workers soon came across fragments of clay tablets covered with cuneiform—the wedge-writing developed in Mesopotamia. Many of these clay tablets were in an unknown tongue. But some were written in *Akkadian* (the language of the Babylonians), a language that Winckler could understand. Akkadian was used by many people in the ancient Near East for diplomacy and trade, much the way English is used worldwide today.

One hot day in August, Professor Winckler solved the mystery of the ruined city. A workman handed him a newly unearthed clay tablet. It was covered with Akkadian cuneiform. As Winckler began to read it, his jaw dropped. Incredibly, not just the language, but the words were familiar. On the tablet was inscribed a translation of the treaty between Pharaoh Ramses II and the Hittite king Hattusilis III, the same treaty that was carved on a temple wall in Egypt 700 miles away! Only the king of the Hittites would have reason to keep such a tablet. Professor Winckler knew he must be digging among the records of the king.

Professor Winckler knew for sure then that he was digging in an ancient Hittite city—and not just any city, but the capital, *Hattusas* (ha-TOO-sass). The powerful Hittites were not based in Syria, as some had believed. They were based in Turkey. Winckler had made one of the most significant discoveries in modern archaeology. The important problem of translating the Hittite tablets remained.

▲   ▲   ▲

The Hittites lived three thousand years ago in a hilly, forested land in southwestern Asia, where the country Turkey is today. Sometimes we call this region Anatolia or Asia Minor. Winters were snowy and cold, the wind roaring over the cliffs of their capital, Hattusas. Summers were hot.

For thousands of years the Hittites were completely forgotten. Yet for more than two hundred years these warlike people were one of the most powerful cultures in the ancient Near East.

The land's original inhabitants were not Hittites. Sometime between 3000 and 2000 B.C. newcomers came into central Anatolia from southern Russia. They settled there—perhaps peacefully, perhaps not. The land they moved into was called Hatti by the people already living there. We call those earlier people Hattians and the newcomers Hittites. The Hittites adopted some gods and religious rituals from the Hattians, and took many of their words into their own language.

Between 1400 and 1200 B.C., the Hittites ruled over countries south and east of their land. They were one of the great powers in the ancient Near East, along with Egypt, Mesopotamia, and a kingdom called *Mitanni* (Mi-TAH-nee). (Mitanni lay between Hatti

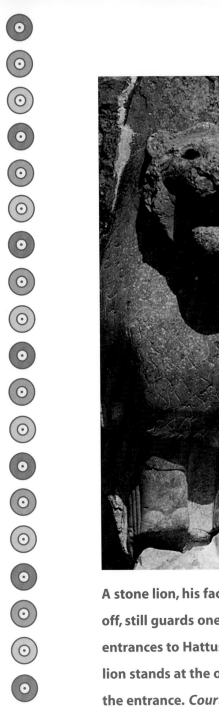

A stone lion, his face half worn off, still guards one of the entrances to Hattusas. Another lion stands at the other side of the entrance. *Courtesy of Erica Schrack*

and Mesopotamia; its people worshipped the storm god *Teshub* and spoke a language called Hurrian.) Sometimes the Hittites fought against the Egyptians and Mesopotamians over territory. Other times they lived in peace with them, and members of the royal families married. Some years after signing the peace treaty with Hattusilis III of the Hittites, Ramses II married Hattusilis's daughter.

Historians divide the history of central Anatolia, home of the Hittites, into different periods. The period before the first Hittite kingdom is called the Assyrian Trading Colony Period. In this period, beginning around 1950 B.C., people from Assyria founded a trading colony in the Anatolian city of Kanesh (ka-NESH). Assyrian traders used it as a home base while they peacefully traded with different cities. Hittites were living in Kanesh and other city-states in Anatolia. Because the early Hittites didn't write, scholars know little about them. Historians know more about the Assyrian traders, who left many business records: what they traded, where they stayed, and even what they paid to rent a donkey!

The next period, between 1750 B.C. and 1450 B.C., is called the Old Hittite Kingdom. Different Hittite city-states struggled for power. Around 1650 B.C. a man called Hattusilis I—which means "man of Hattusas"—claimed Hattusas as his capital. He conquered many surrounding cities in Anatolia and united them. He was the first true Hittite king.

The final period of Hittite history was the Hittite Empire, from about 1450 B.C. until just after 1200 B.C. In this period Hittite power was at its peak. The Hittites defeated the powerful kingdom of Mitanni to the east and conquered much of Syria. The widow of King Tut in Egypt even asked the Hittite king Suppiluliumas (soo-pi-lu-LYOO-mas) to send her his son in marriage. The king was so surprised he wrote back, "This kind of thing has never happened to me before!" He sent his son to meet the queen. Unfortunately, the prince was killed before he met his bride.

From pictures, we know some Hittites had straight black hair and lighter skin. They wore colorful clothing of linen and wool and shoes with turned-up toes.

Hittite culture adopted much from the Mesopotamians. Hittite scribes wrote on clay tablets in cuneiform learned from the Babylonians. They adopted many Mesopotamian laws as well. For example, a Mesopotamian law said that a man who injures a rented ox must replace it. The Hittites wrote a similiar law for themselves. They sometimes used cylinder seals like the Mesopotamians, too.

Other aspects of the Hittite culture were common to many people in the region. Like the Egyptians and Mesopotamians, the Hittites raised sheep, goats, and cattle and grew ancient kinds of wheat and barley, as well as chickpeas, onions, garlic, and cucumbers. The Hittites combined these foods into stews, soups, and dozens of kinds of bread.

The Hittites developed their own styles of art, carving bold figures with big heads into rock walls and cliffs over springs. They celebrated their own holidays, including a 38-day festival in the spring named for an edible plant. They spoke their own language, distantly related to English.

These low gray rocky walls mark the rooms and buildings of Hattusas, the once-great capital of the Hittite empire. Half buried in the dirt are large clay storage vessels that might have held offerings of grain, or perhaps oil, for the gods. *Courtesy of Erica Schrack*

The Hittites worshipped so many gods that they called themselves "people of a thousand gods." Although warlike, they were open to foreign religions. They worshipped foreign gods along with Hittite ones.

Surrounding the Hittites were other Anatolian cultures, many of them enemies of the Hittites. The Kaskans lived to the north, frequently crossing Hittite borders to steal cattle and burn farmlands. To the south and southwest lived the Luwians, who spoke a related language and who carved their own kind of hieroglyphs on stone. For a long time scholars referred to these as Hittite hieroglyphs, not realizing they were written in a different language. To the south and east lived other cultures: the people of Kizzuwadna and the people of Mitanni, a powerful kingdom the Hittites destroyed in war.

In 1200 B.C. waves of invaders from the west attacked Hatti and other countries in the Near East. Among the invaders were the Philistines, who gave their name to the land of Palestine. The invaders crossed the Aegean (a-JEE-un) Sea to Anatolia and other lands. The Egyptians called the invaders the Peoples of the Sea because many of them came by boat. Only the Egyptians managed to stop their onslaught and defend themselves.

Around the time of the invasion, the capital of the Hittites was burned and the people defeated. Some historians think the Hittites' northern neighbors, the Kaskans, took advantage of the invasion and destroyed Hatti. Whoever was responsible, around 1200 B.C. the Hittite Empire came to an end.

Hittite Architecture

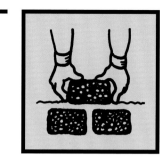

This is a view from inside the secret tunnel into the walled city of Hattusas.

Living in a forested land, the Hittites had wood to use for building. They built their homes of mud brick or stone, often using wood for upper stories. Usually the floors were dirt. The Hittites sometimes covered the dirt with plaster, pebbles, or flat rocks called flagstone. Stone staircases covered with plaster sometimes connected floors. Houses might contain several rooms—a storeroom filled with large clay jars, a kitchen with a hearth and oven, and other rooms for sleeping or working. Some rooms may have been bathrooms. The Hittites used clay bathtubs, in adult and child sizes. Some of the tubs had built-in seats.

In the capital, Hattusas, thick stone walls surrounded houses, temples, and the royal palace. The houses stood beside paved alleys or roads. Ditches next to the roads drained rainwater. Eight gates led into the city. The gates were locked each night and opened in the morning. Stone lions guarded one gate. Twin stone sphinxes protected another. On a third gate a carved stone soldier—perhaps a god—carried a battle-ax and a sword.

This is the outside view of the Postern Gate, the entrance to the secret tunnel into the walled city of Hattusas. Hittite soldiers went through this tunnel to attack enemies who were besieging them around the city.

In this wall carving, a Hittite king and queen worship the storm god, who is represented by his sacred animal, the bull. The king wears a long robe and a close-fitting cap. You can see his *lituus,* the curved staff at his side. The queen wears a long skirt. Both wear earrings and shoes with turned-up toes. *Courtesy of Museum of Anatolian Civilizations, Ankara*

A secret tunnel lay under one of the city walls. The Hittites used this tunnel for surprise attacks if enemies besieged the city. Today, this tunnel still exists—it is possible to walk through it, tracing the steps of the ancient soldiers.

Inside the palace of Hattusas were many rooms, including the king's archives—storehouses for thousands of clay tablets. In ancient times,

These carvings of running gods appear at a sacred Hittite site that is now called Yazilikaya, near Hattusas.

the tablets rested on wooden shelves, much as books line shelves in modern libraries. More than twenty temples to different gods stood in the city. The Great Temple was the largest. It was a fitting home for Hatti's most important god and goddess: the storm god Teshub and the sun goddess of Arinna.

The Great Temple was really two buildings. The temple itself contained an inner court-yard, many small rooms, and one or two larger rooms that held the images of the gods.

This temple building stood in a yard completely surrounded by the second building, which was two or three stories tall. This second building contained storerooms for the offerings the Hittites brought their gods. The priests, singers, and scribes that worked in the temple lived in a third building across the street.

Maze of the Great Temple

Pretend you are a temple servant around 1250 B.C. One of the priests asks you to run some errands inside the Great Temple. See if you can find your way from room to room, using only your finger, and find a way out of the temple. (Note: enter rooms only through the tiny white boxes indicating doorways.)

Materials

▲ *Plan of the Great Temple, including the temple itself, the surrounding storerooms, and the staff living quarters on the next page*

Directions

1. Start in the yard within the outer storeroom building, by the basin. Make sure the basin is clean. After all, this is where the king, queen, and high officials wash during religious ceremonies before entering the temple building.

2. Find the doorways that will take you into storeroom 10. You will have to go through several other rooms to get there. Fetch a clay tablet from room 10.

3. Take the clay tablet to room 82. An official needs it to check off some offerings that just came from a Hittite landowner.

4. Now go to room 64 to meet a new singer from the land of the Hurrians, a neighboring country. This singer just arrived at the temple today and needs your help.

5. The new singer thinks he left his *sistrum* (a sort of tambourine) in room 15 when he had his temple tour this morning. Go look for it.

6. The sistrum isn't there. Go to one of the guardrooms, 1c, near the main entrance to the outer courtyard. Ask the guard in room 1c if he's seen it.

7. The guard thinks he saw a sistrum in room 41, next to one of the giant clay storage jars, which are half-buried in the floor.

8. Go to room 41. The sistrum is there, leaning against a huge jar that contains oil for religious offerings.

9. Take the sistrum back to room 64. But the singer is gone!

10. Go to the temple staff's living quarters to look for the singer. Exit the temple between rooms 64 and 71a. Cross the street and enter the staff's living quarters.

11. The singer is standing in the courtyard inside the staff's living quarters. You give him the sistrum. He thanks you in the Hurrian language. You return to the courtyard near the basin.

As you continue reading about the Hittites you'll learn about sistra, why large jars were buried in the floor, and more.

Inside the Great Temple, Hittite priests and royalty performed rituals to their most important deities, the storm god Teshub and the sun goddess of Arinna. Images of the goddess and god probably stood in two small rooms inside the central building. *Courtesy of Gebrüder Mann Verlag, Berlin, Kurt Bittel, Bogazköy IV, Berlin*

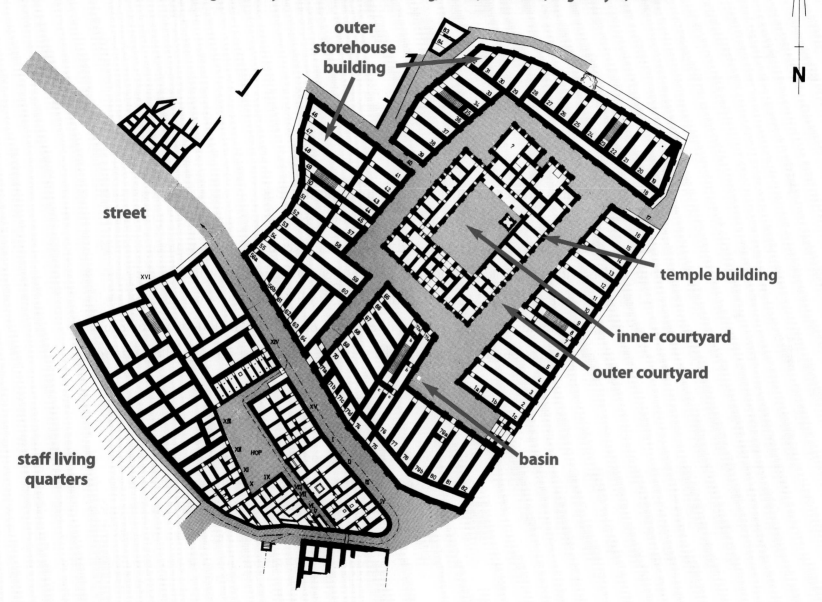

outer storehouse building

street

staff living quarters

temple building

inner courtyard

outer courtyard

basin

N

Hittite Clothing

Hittites dressed simply in wool or linen clothes. Both men and women wore tunics: garments like shirts coming down to the knees or ankles. The tunics had long or short sleeves and no buttons. Over their tunics, women covered themselves with a long piece of cloth, wrapping themselves from their hair to their ankles when they went outdoors. Men often wore cloaks. Both men and women fastened their clothes at the shoulders with fancy pins, often made of bronze. The king wore long robes, leather shoes, and a round cap. He carried a stick like a shepherd's crook, called a *lituus* (li-TOO-us).

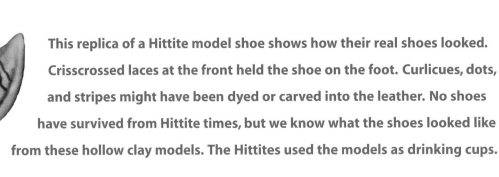

This replica of a Hittite model shoe shows how their real shoes looked. Crisscrossed laces at the front held the shoe on the foot. Curlicues, dots, and stripes might have been dyed or carved into the leather. No shoes have survived from Hittite times, but we know what the shoes looked like from these hollow clay models. The Hittites used the models as drinking cups.

Jewelry was common. Men and women wore rings, necklaces, bracelets, anklets, and earrings. Even little girls wore earrings in pierced ears. Jewelry was made of silver, gold, bronze, and more rarely, iron. Today we use iron for making frying pans and gates, but in the days of the Hittites, iron was very precious. People in the Near East had not yet succeeded in working well with iron. Most metal objects were made of bronze, which needed different tools and techniques. The Hittites had managed to work with small amounts of iron, but with difficulty. The iron was very valuable—but probably made heavy jewelry.

Many people wore pendants around their necks. These were usually made of metal shaped into people, gods, suns, animals, or even pairs of shoes. The Hittites may have believed the pendants acted as amulets or lucky charms to protect them.

Hittite Shoes

Here's a project that will curl your toes. See the shortcut at the end if you don't want to sew.

Adult help recommended for the sewing.

Materials

- ▲ 1 old pair socks
- ▲ 1-foot-square piece vinyl (available in fabric stores)
- ▲ Markers
- ▲ Scissors
- ▲ 6 straight pins
- ▲ Needle
- ▲ Nylon thread

Directions

1. Put on your old socks. Turn the vinyl face down on the floor and stand on it. With a dark marker, carefully trace around each foot onto the vinyl.

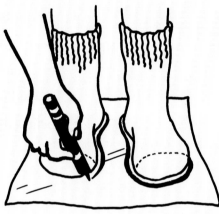

2. Step off the vinyl. Mark a dot on the vinyl, centered, about two inches above the toes of each sock. Draw two diagonal lines from the dot to the top edges of the sock, forming a triangle.

3. Cut the vinyl around the outer edge of the pattern outline including the triangle above the sock toes.

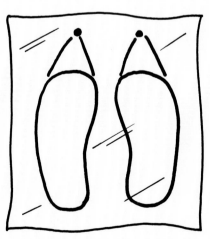

4. Before you take off each sock, draw a line on the sock around the edge of the bottom of each foot. (This tickles!)

5. Place one vinyl sole face down on the table. Match the heel of one sock to the heel of the vinyl. Make sure the middle of the sock heel is right on top of the middle of the vinyl heel. Pin the middle of these two heels together. Stretch the sock so that you can pin the tip of the vinyl toe to the tip of the sock. The vinyl sole is longer than the sock so it will make a curve. Pin the rest of the vinyl sole to the sock. Try to make the markings on the sock line up closely with the edge of the vinyl.

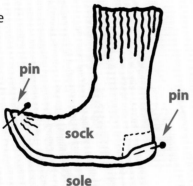

pin

pin

sock

sole

6. Thread the needle and tie the two ends of the thread together in a strong knot.

7. Sew the vinyl sole to the sock. Take out each pin as you sew around the sock. When you come near the end of a piece of thread, knot it and cut it off. Continue with another knotted piece of thread.

8. Make the other shoe.

9. **Optional** Decorate the socks with markers, making designs like the ones pictured.

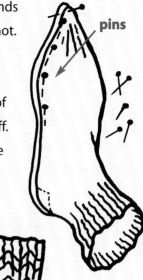

pins

Shortcut

If you don't have time to sew the soles on the socks, just do steps 1–3. Take off your socks and slide the vinyl soles inside. Decorate the socks and then put them back on.

shortcut vinyl sole

151

Hittite Costume

You can dress like a Hittite with a long shirt, safety pins, and a tablecloth or pillowcase for a veil or cloak. Try combining these with the Hittite shoes and pendant.

Materials

▲ Long T-shirt or other shirt without buttons

▲ Belt (optional)

▲ Piece of colored cloth, about 3 by 4 feet for boys and 4 feet square for girls

▲ 1 or 2 safety pins

▲ Hittite shoes

▲ Pendant or other jewelry such as rings, bracelets, and earrings (Try the gold earrings from the Nubian king/queen costume.)

Directions

Put on the shirt. It should come at least to your knees. Take off your pants, but leave on your underwear. The Hittites wore underwear, which they called *kaluppa*. Add a belt if you like.

For a boy's outfit, drape the cloth over the back, then fasten the cloth to the front of the T-shirt shoulders using the safety pins. For a girl's outfit, fasten the cloth loosely around the neck with a single safety pin. Pull up the part behind your shoulders so it forms a hood.

Put on your Hittite shoes. Put on your pendant and other jewelry. Wear your hair loose and pushed back behind your ears, just like the Hittites.

Hittite Pendant

You can make a pendant like ones the Hittites wore. You can wear it with your Hittite costume.

Materials

- ▲ 1 piece thin cardboard, at least 4 to 5 inches long on each side
- ▲ Pencil or pen
- ▲ Craft knife or scissors
- ▲ 1 4-inch-square piece gold or silver foil or origami paper (from an art supply or craft store)
- ▲ Glue stick
- ▲ Hole puncher
- ▲ Piece of string or a thin chain

This small gold pendant was an amulet or charm, to be worn around the neck for good luck. If you look closely, you can see horns on the hat. The horns show that it is the image of a god. In Hittite art, only gods wore hats like this one. *Copyright The British Museum, London*

Directions

Copy the god design in the photograph onto the cardboard. Carefully cut around the design using the craft knife or scissors. Use the pencil or pen to lightly trace around your design onto the back side of the gold or silver foil. Now turn your cardboard design over and trace around it again, on another part of the foil. Cut out the two pieces of foil and glue them to the cardboard, one on each side. Punch a hole near the top of the foil-covered cardboard. Slide your string or chain through the hole. Fasten it around your neck.

Hittites decorated their clothing with stripes and other designs, and sometimes tassels.

Hittite Writing

The Hittites lived long before anyone in the world spoke English. Even so, their language was distantly related to ours—as well as to German, Latin, Spanish, and Russian. Scholars didn't know this originally. Before Hittite was translated, most scholars were certain that Hittite was part of a different family of languages—a family that included Arabic and Hebrew, and the Babylonian language Akkadian. One man's creativity led him to a different answer—which proved to be right.

▲   ▲   ▲

When Hugo Winckler uncovered the city of Hattusas, he discovered thousands of clay tablets covered with cuneiform writing. Cuneiform was the writing system developed in Mesopotamia. The Hittites learned it from the Babylonians and used it to write in their own language.

At first scholars could read only a few words in Hittite cuneiform; most they could not understand. It was a bit like trying to read a foreign language written in your own alphabet. You can try to pronounce the words, but you can't understand what they mean.

Hittite Hieroglyphs

The Hittites wrote in two different ways: in cuneiform (wedge-writing), and also in a special kind of hieroglyphs (picture-writing). Scholars called the picture-writing "Hittite hieroglyphs." It took a long time for scholars to realize that it wasn't just the two writing systems that were different. The languages being written were different, too. When the Hittites wrote in cuneiform, they used the Hittite language. But when they wrote in hieroglyphs, they used a different language called *Luwian* (LOO-we-an). Luwian was spoken by many Hittites as well as by their Luwian neighbors to the south and southwest. The two languages were very similar.

Luwian hieroglyphs look nothing like the hieroglyphs used in Egypt or Nubia. The animal heads, squiggles, and geometric shapes almost always appear on rock carvings or seals.

A few years after Professor Winckler began to dig in Hattusas, a scholar named Friedrich Hrozny (ROZ-nee) set out to translate Hittite cuneiform. He looked first at the words he could understand. One was the symbol for bread. Many cultures in the ancient Near East used the same symbol to write the word "bread." Although the Sumerians pronounced the symbol *ninda*, others used it to stand for the word "bread" in their own languages. When Professor Hrozny saw the symbol, he knew the sentence was about bread.

When Hrozny sounded out the sentence, this is what he came up with: *Nu NINDA-an e-iz-za-at-te-ni wa-a-tar-ma e-ku-ut-te-ni*. This sentence looks like nonsense to us. But Hrozny spotted a familiar-looking word, *wa-a-tar*. He thought it might mean "water." Hrozny thought the word *e-iz-za-at-te-ni* sounded a little like the German word *essen*, which means "to eat." He figured that *e-ku-ut-te-ni* meant "to drink." He decided the sentence said, "Then you will eat bread and drink water!" If this was true, then Hittite was related to English, German, and other languages spoken in Europe and India.

Other scholars confirmed Professor Hrozny's findings. Sure enough, Hittite is a member of the language family that includes English—the oldest member of that family to be discovered.

Understanding Hittite

See if you can do what Professor Hrozny did. Try figuring out the meanings of these Hittite words:

kard

tri

pata

Which word means "three"? Which word means "foot"? Which word means "heart"?

Tri means three. Pata means foot. Kard means heart. Did they remind you of any words you know in English or other languages?

Tri is part of the English words triangle and tricycle—one has three angles and the other has three wheels. It is the word for three in many languages related to both English and Hittite, such as Irish and Russian. Tri also sounds like the word three.

Pata is the Spanish word for paw. The Latin word for foot, ped, is part of our word pedestrian (someone who walks on foot). It is also part of the word pedal.

Kard is the word for heart in Latin as well as Hittite. Many English words have parts of this Latin word in them. Think of cardiologist (a heart doctor) and the word electrocardiogram (a medical test on the heart).

Hittite, Latin, Greek, English, Spanish, and many other languages are related. Sometimes you can figure out a word in a foreign language because it sounds similar to one you know in English.

Even though Hittite is related to English, much of its vocabulary comes from the language of the Hattians—the people who lived in the land before the Hittites came. These words sound nothing at all like English, Spanish, or Latin.

Here are some other Hittite words:

seknu means cloak

gapari means tunic

kariulli means hood

patalla means sock

Next, practice saying this useful Hittite sentence:

Ini-mu uttar karuiliyaz piran natta kuwapikki kisat.

It means, "This kind of thing has never happened to me before." You might try saying this in class if your teacher asks you a question you can't answer.

Scribal Schoolwork

Hittites learned to write from the Babylonians, using a form of Babylonian cuneiform. The Hittites wrote on clay tablets and cylinder seals as well as on wooden tablets covered with wax.

Just like the people of other countries of the ancient Near East, most Hittites couldn't read or write. Those who could worked for the government, either in the temples or for the king. There were two kinds of scribes: scribes who wrote on clay tablets, and scribes who wrote on wax-covered wooden tablets.

Hittites learned to be scribes by copying other scribes' work. You can learn to write like the Hittites the same way.

Materials

▲ Pencil
▲ Paper

Directions

Copy the following actual Hittite law. The exact translation is "If a man free nose his someone bites one pound silver gives." It means, "If anyone bites a free man's nose, he pays a pound of silver."

This is a sample of Hittite cuneiform. *Courtesy of Gary Beckman*

Writing on Clay

You can make a *stylus* (a writing instrument) and use it to write on clay.

Adult help recommended with the hacksaw or knife.

Materials

▲ *1 wooden chopstick (the kind where the handle is square and topped off with a little pyramid)*
▲ *Hacksaw or sharp knife*
▲ *Paper plate*
▲ *Self-hardening clay such as Marblex, or potter's clay*

Directions

Cut the chopstick in two. Make your cut through the square handle, near the middle of the chopstick, so that one end forms a square. You'll use this end to press into the clay. On the paper plate, knead the clay and shape it into a flattened circle or square.

Practice making wedges by pressing the square end of the chopstick into the clay at an angle with your right hand so that you get a triangle shape with the thin tail made by the chopstick's edge. (If you use your left hand, the wedges will come out backward.) Press just once for each wedge—don't try to write as you would with a pencil. Experiment with different angles to form the four kinds of wedges below.

Now make one final kind of wedge. This one looks a little like an angelfish. Hold the stylus nearly upright. Press the left corner into the clay.

Erase your tablet with a wet finger or by kneading. Try copying the law from page 157, using your stylus in wet clay. Now you can really write like a Hittite—or a Mesopotamian!

Hittite Work

The Hittites shared many ways of living and working with other people in the ancient Near East. Farming was the most common way of life. Even people who had another job spent part of the year farming.

There were also craftspeople, especially in towns. These included basket weavers, cloth makers, carpenters, stone masons, potters, leather workers, tailors, and copper workers. Royalty and wealthy people could hire the services of gold- and silversmiths, gem cutters, shoemakers, and people who made leggings or socks.

Other people worked as servants or slaves. They had some rights, but not many. One law said that a servant who annoyed his master could be killed or injured. Servants worked in the households of wealthy Hittites. In many ways they were no better off than slaves. Some of these servants were foreign captives brought back from wars.

Like the Mesopotamians, the Hittites made use of several different professions if they became ill. Women worked as midwives delivering babies. Physicians treated illness, as did sorcerers and sorceresses, who performed rituals to heal people of ailments.

Sometimes people with problems went to a special person called an "Old Woman," a woman who used magic to heal people. Commonly, an Old Woman mixed together colored wool, clay, food, and sometimes animal dung. Sometimes she made little images of the patient with this mixture. Other times she spread the mixture onto the person's body. Then she'd say what she wanted to happen. For example, an Old Woman might say, "Just as this dung is drying up, so may the evil inside you dry up and go away!"

We don't know if the patients treated by an Old Woman ever got better. Probably some of them were going to get better anyway. Perhaps believing in the magic helped some of them feel better faster.

No matter what type of work a person performed, life centered around the seasons. Planting grain, harvesting, and storing food were all very important.

Soldier's Work

Soldiers protected the land and people of Hatti from attackers. They stood watch in the towns along the borders. Soldiers also fought in battles in other countries. King Suppiluliumas, King Muwatallis (moo-wa-TAL-lis), and other kings frequently led their soldiers to war in other lands. If the Hittites won, they might leave the conquered people in peace but bring the leaders back to Hatti as prisoners. Sometimes the Hittites would bring back ordinary citizens of the other country, to be servants or citizens in Hatti. All of this was common practice in Egypt and Mesopotamia as well as among the Hittites.

The Hittites would often install a ruler of their choice—sometimes a relative of the

Hittite king—to rule over the land they conquered. Most often the new ruler was a member of the royal family who had been defeated. Often these new rulers, or their children, married a member of the Hittite royal family.

The conquered lands were called *tributaries*. The Hittites expected them to be loyal to the Hittites—and to pay taxes to them. The new ruler had to sign a treaty agreeing to many conditions. For instance, he was required to return to Hatti any Hittite who fled to his country. To make sure the new ruler upheld the conditions, the Hittites summoned their thousand gods to witness the treaty. If the signer broke the treaty, the gods who witnessed it were supposed to wipe out the signer and his family. If he upheld the treaty, the signer was promised to live to an old age. The names of the gods, the blessings, and the curses were listed in the treaty. Obviously the Hittites intended to frighten the new ruler into keeping his agreement.

Combat

Dressed in short kilts with belts, helmets, and boots, many Hittite soldiers fought on foot, wielding bronze swords. Others battled from war chariots, wearing ankle-length coats of scale armor. Teams of specially trained horses pulled the Hittite war chariots into battle. Three men rode on each chariot: a warrior, a guard, and a driver. While the chariot dipped and plunged, the warrior shot arrows at enemy soldiers or thrust at them with his sword. The guard held a shield protecting the warrior. The driver, shielded only by the front of the chariot, guided the team of horses. Screams of dying horses and men filled the air.

One of the most famous battles in Hittite and Egyptian history was fought near a city called Qadesh (Ka-DESH), far south of Hatti in modern Syria. Qadesh and the surrounding countries were tributaries of the Hittites. When Ramses II was pharaoh of Egypt, one of these countries, Amurru, decided to ally with Egypt, which angered the Hittites.

In 1275 B.C. the Hittite king Muwatallis brought a large army to Qadesh to fight the Egyptians for control of the area. He knew that Ramses II was bringing the Egyptian army north to attack his army. Muwatallis knew that the Egyptians knew that the Hittite army was waiting for them. To increase the chances of Hittite victory, he devised a plan. The plan is famous today as one of the first recorded examples of *subterfuge* (sneakiness) in battle.

Muwatallis sent a spy south to meet the Egyptian army with special instructions to let himself be captured and to give misleading battle plan information when questioned. This must have taken tremendous courage on the part of the spy. When the Egyptians captured him and questioned him, the spy followed his instructions and told the Egyptians misleading information. He told the Egyptians that the Hittites were far away to the north. In fact, the Hittites were hidden behind the nearby city of Qadesh.

Thinking they were safe, the first part of Egypt's army rushed past Qadesh. As the Egyptians passed the city, the Hittite chariots attacked. Many Egyptians died.

The Hittites would have won the battle easily if they had stayed battle ready. But the soldiers began to loot the pharaoh's camp. Meanwhile another group of Egyptian soldiers arrived and attacked. The Hittites fought hard and many people died on both sides.

After the battle, Ramses II boasted that the Egyptians had won. He was so proud of his own bravery that he had scenes from the battle carved on the temple he built in Nubia, Abu Simbel. In his inscriptions he called King Muwatallis a coward. In fact, the Hittites killed half the Egyptians and chased the rest off the battlefield. They controlled Qadesh and the surrounding countries after the battle.

Both sides claimed they won even though each army lost many soldiers.

Is there another way to resolve conflicts where both sides come away feeling like they've won? Think of a conflict you were involved in (or you saw) where both you and the other side felt like winners. This is a difficult task. It takes great skill at diplomacy to bring off a real double-sided victory.

Diplomacy

The Hittites used other techniques besides war to maintain relations with their neighbors. Letters of peace, sent with gifts, were common between ruling families. A noblewoman named Puduhepas (pu-du-HE-pas) wrote such a letter. Puduhepas was the wife of a man named Hattusilis, the brother of King Muwatallis. Hattusilis later became the Hittite king Hattusilis III.

Some years after the battle of Qadesh, Puduhepas wrote to Ramses II's wife Nefertare (ne-fer-TA-re) explaining her hopes for a relationship of peace and brotherhood between the kings of the two countries. In response, Nefertare sent Puduhepas a gold necklace and 12 fine linen garments along with her own wishes for peace.

Hittite Food

To the Hittites, bread and water were the staples of life. One king wrote advice to this son, Mursilis, adding, "So keep your father's words. As long as you keep them, you shall eat bread and drink water."

Bread, Bread, and More Bread

Like other ancient people in this book, the Hittites baked bread from barley flour or wheat. They used emmer wheat, and at least one other ancient kind of wheat. Bread was their most important food. Here is a list of some of the different kinds of Hittite bread.

Thick bread	Bread with oil	Emmer bread	Dark loaves
Thin bread	Runner's bread	Fresh bread	Red loaves
Sour bread	Soldier's bread	Stale bread	Bread made in
Sweet bread	Barley bread	Moist bread	different towns
Honey bread	Bread from chickpea	Long loaves	Daily bread
Fat bread	flour	Little loaves	Table bread

Hittite bakers made bread in many different shapes, too.

Round loaves

Loaves shaped like teeth

Loaves shaped like tongues

Loaves shaped like a mouth, tongue, and 12 teeth

Loaves shaped like cattle and sheep

Loaves shaped like nails

Loaves shaped like birds

Loaves shaped like hands

Loaves shaped like piglets

Loaves shaped like the sun, moon, and stars

These fancy kinds of bread were mostly for kings or gods. Think of all the different kinds of bread you've eaten in your life. Include sweet breads like cinnamon rolls, and bread in different shapes, like tortillas or bagels. How does your list compare to the Hittites' list?

Pig's Milk and Other Goodies

Besides bread, the Hittites ate meat from lambs, pigs, cattle, and goats. They made cheese, yogurt, and maybe whipped cream using milk from goats or pigs. If they used cows' milk, they didn't mention it in their writings. Can you imagine—whipped cream made from pig's milk?

The Hittites rounded out their diet with cucumbers, onions, garlic, and fruits such as grapes, apricots, apples, and figs. They also ate chickpeas, beans, and lentils. They seasoned their foods with cumin, coriander, salt, and sesame seeds. They made soups and stews, which they served their kings and gods. They didn't leave recipes.

The Hittites drank beer, which they made from barley, and wine, which they made from grapes. Sometimes they put honey in their beer or wine. They also drank water and milk from pigs or goats.

They didn't eat potatoes, tomatoes, chicken, or chicken eggs. These foods didn't exist in their country—or elsewhere in the ancient Near East.

Storing Food in the Ground

People throughout the ancient Near East stored grain and liquids in large clay jars. These jars often had curved bottoms, so they couldn't stand upright well. The Hittites and other ancient people often buried the jars in dirt floors. The upper parts of the jars were above ground.

The Hittites filled the jars in the fall and opened them to bring out the food in the spring. In between, the tops of the jars were sealed. To seal a jar, they covered the stopper with wet clay. Then they pressed a stamp seal or rolled a cylinder seal on the clay. If anyone cracked open the seal, people would know.

You can store food Hittite-style for the winter. Open up your jars in the spring.

Materials

▲ Cardboard shoebox or other small box without lid

▲ 6 cups dirt

▲ 3 small empty glass jars with lids, like baby food, mustard, and artichoke heart jars

wet clay

▲ $^1/_4$ to $^1/_2$ cup cooking oil

▲ $^1/_4$ to $^1/_2$ cup whole wheat berries or pearl barley

▲ $^1/_4$ to $^1/_2$ cup dried peas, lentils, or beans

▲ $^1/_4$ cup self-hardening clay such as Marblex, or potter's clay

▲ Cylinder seal (from Mesopotamian section) or rubber stamp

Directions

Fill the box half full of dirt. Pack the dirt in firmly.

Next, fill the glass jars—one with oil, one with grain, and the third with dried peas, lentils, or beans. Place the lids on top and close tightly.

Seal the jars. Cover the lid and neck of each jar with a thin layer of clay. Now press the stamp or roll the seal on the moist clay. Set each jar into the dirt so the top half or third is uncovered.

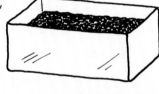

You can use your cylinder seal to make an impression in the clay.

Hittite Hummus

This recipe uses Hittite ingredients to make a tasty spread or dip.

Adult help recommended with the blender.

Ingredients

▲ *1 can chickpeas (sometimes called garbanzo beans)*

▲ *2 tablespoons tahini (sometimes called sesame seed paste)*

▲ *¹/₂ teaspoon salt*

▲ *¹/₂ teaspoon cumin*

▲ *1 tablespoon apple juice*

▲ *3 tablespoons water*

▲ *¹/₄ teaspoon garlic powder*

▲ *Sliced cucumbers or bread*

Utensils

▲ *Can opener*

▲ *Colander*

▲ *Large bowl*

▲ *Fork, blender, or potato masher*

▲ *Spoon or fork for stirring*

▲ *Measuring spoons*

▲ *Knife and cutting board for cucumbers (optional)*

Directions

Open the can of chickpeas and place them in a colander in the kitchen sink until most of the liquid drains out. Transfer them to a large bowl. Mash the chickpeas using a fork, blender, or potato masher. First stir, then add two tablespoons tahini to the chickpeas (oil sometimes separates and rests on top of the tahini). Add the salt and cumin to the bowl and stir well. Finally add the apple juice, water, and garlic powder, and stir until completely mixed. To eat, spread the hummus on bread or cucumber slices.

Hittite Lentil Soup

T he Hittites may have eaten a soup like this during their cold winters.

Adult help recommended with the stove.

Ingredients

- ▲ 2 tablespoons olive oil
- ▲ 1 medium onion, chopped
- ▲ 1 teaspoon salt
- ▲ 1 clove garlic, minced or crushed (or ⅛ teaspoon garlic powder)
- ▲ 4 cups water (You may substitute 1 cup beef broth for 1 cup water.)
- ▲ ½ cup raw lentils, rinsed and free of little pebbles
- ▲ ¾ teaspoon ground cumin
- ▲ ½ cup raw pearl barley (optional)

Utensils

- ▲ Cutting board
- ▲ Sharp knife
- ▲ Large pot or frying pan
- ▲ Stove
- ▲ Measuring spoons
- ▲ Large spoon for stirring
- ▲ Measuring cup
- ▲ Garlic press (optional)

Directions

Before you start cooking, chase any dogs or pigs from your kitchen. Pour the olive oil in the pot and heat over a medium flame. (Be careful not to burn the oil.) Add the chopped onion. Cook until the onion begins to look clear (translucent). Add the garlic or garlic powder and cook another one to two minutes. Add the water, lentils, salt, and cumin. Add the barley now if you are using it. Bring the soup to a boil. (You may raise the heat to do this.) Turn the heat to low and simmer about 45 minutes, stirring occasionally. The soup is ready when you can easily squish the lentils with a spoon. Enjoy your feast—fit for a god!

Kitchen Rules

Servants cooked the meals for the royal family, following special rules. One rule stated that no dogs or pigs were allowed to roam in the king's kitchen. This rule was for cleanliness.

Hittite Religion

In the land of the thousand gods, the chief deities were the sun goddess of Arinna and the storm god. Also called *Hebat*, the sun goddess sometimes appears with her sacred animal, the lion. The sacred animal of Teshub, the storm god, was the bull.

Besides their own gods, the Hittites adopted the gods of other lands. They worshipped the Mesopotamian goddess Ishtar, and the god Ea. Many villages had their own special gods.

The Hittites believed that their welfare depended on their gods and their gods depended on them. Without the gods, for example, the Hittites believed that plants wouldn't grow and animals and people wouldn't have babies. Without people to give offerings, the gods would starve.

This hollow bull's head was used during religious ceremonies. It was used to pour drink-offerings to the storm god. *Courtesy of Museum of Anatolian Civilizations, Ankara*

In many ways, Hittite religion was like other religions in the ancient Near East. Priests and priestesses staffed temples for a particular god or goddess. They led rituals every day. They took in food offerings and ate any food that was left over after it was offered to the gods. They took care of the image of the god or goddess, washing it and dressing it daily. During special holidays, they brought the god's image outside the temple for a procession to a sacred place.

Anatolian Sistrum

During their holidays, the Hittites feasted and told myths. Sometimes they acted out pretend battles. Musicians played sacred music. They beat drums, clanged cymbals, and played stringed instruments. One of the instruments they played was a kind of tambourine we call a sistrum. The Egyptians and other ancient peoples also played a kind of sistrum.

You can make a sistrum you can really play. Because no examples of Hittite sistra have survived, this one is modeled after a bronze sistrum made by people in Anatolia before the Hittites came to power.

This is a replica of a musical instrument called a sistrum, made by the people who lived in Hatti before the Hittites. Across the ancient Near East, priestesses shook instruments like this one at religious ceremonies.

Adult help recommended with the scissors or shears.

Materials

▲ *Small sturdy cardboard box or lid, about 4 to 5 inches long on at least 2 sides (Boxes for notecards or chocolates are good.)*
▲ *Hole puncher*
▲ *3 chopsticks (not the pull-apart kind)*
▲ *Ruler*
▲ *Pen or pencil*
▲ *Strong scissors or kitchen shears*
▲ *8 to 16 metal washers (from a hardware store)*
▲ *Duct tape*

Directions

Punch a hole in the middle of one side of the box. If the box is rectangular, use one of the long sides. Punch a second hole in the opposite side, directly across from the first. (You may need help if the cardboard is thick.) Try pushing a chopstick through the two holes, narrow end first. Remove the chopstick. On one of the sides not yet punched, punch two holes about one inch

apart. Repeat this step on the opposite side, punching holes directly across from the first set. When you are done, two sides should have one hole, and two sides should have two holes each. The sides with one hole will be the top and bottom of the sistrum.

If your box is less than an inch deep, you need to cut a piece out of the back to make room for the washers. Draw a line on the

cut out

back of the box about ½ inch from the edge, all the way around. Cut out this shape. Push the narrow end of a chopstick through one of the two side holes. String four to eight washers on the tip of the chopstick.

Push the chopstick through the other hole directly across. Keep pushing until the chopstick gets stuck. If the holes are too wide or your chopstick too narrow to stay on its own,

secure outside ends with duct tape. Repeat this process with another chopstick strung through the remaining two holes.

Arrange the washers so that half are on the left, and half on the right. Decide which side will be the top and which will be the bottom of the sistrum. Coming up from the bottom, push the narrow end of the last chopstick through the two remaining holes. Leave several inches of the chopstick at the bottom for a handle. Secure with duct tape if necessary. Now you're ready to shake your sistrum.

tape if needed

tape if needed

Conclusion

Sometime shortly after 1200 B.C. the Hittite Empire collapsed, when the Peoples of the Sea invaded many countries in the ancient Near East. The Hittites were weakened by shortages of food. They had many enemies around them, including the Kaskans to the north. Perhaps it was the Kaskans who attacked the capital Hattusas, which was consumed by a great fire. Many Hittite towns were abandoned as their people fled to nearby lands.

But the Hittite culture did not die out completely. In lands outside Hatti that had once been ruled by the Hittites, parts of the culture survived. After a period of chaos, new kingdoms arose in Syria. Their kings wrote in Hittite hieroglyphs using the Luwian language. They also wore shoes with upturned toes. Scholars call these people the Neo-Hittites, which means "New Hittites."

For five centuries after the Hittite Empire ended, the Neo-Hittites kept parts of the Hittite culture alive. Then all traces of the Hittites vanished from human memory. Only mysterious carvings and ruins on a hillside remained, until scholars unearthed the secrets of this great and powerful people.

Epilogue

The Egyptians did not live alone in the ancient Near East. Many different cultures shared their world. Nubia lay directly south. Mesopotamia lay to the northeast in Asia. The Hittites lived to the northwest, in what is now Turkey. All these cultures communicated, traded, and sometimes fought with Egypt.

Besides these cultures, others loomed large in the Egyptians' world. Libya bordered the desert west of the Nile. The mysterious land of Punt lay to the southeast, source of spices, incense, and baboons. Syria and Canaan lay along the seacoast between Egypt and Mesopotamia. The Israelites, Philistines, and Phoenicians settled there, among other peoples. Ships roamed the Mediterranean from the islands of Greece, Cyprus, and Crete. Cultures known mostly by historians, Ebla, Mitanni, and Susa, flourished and died during Egypt's 3,000-year history.

Farther afield, the lands of India and China birthed rich civilizations. People lived in other parts of Africa and in Europe, too. Unknown to the Egyptians, civilizations grew in the Americas, and cultures developed in Australia.

Ancient Egypt had much in common with its neighbors, the Mesopotamians, Nubians, and other nearby peoples. They raised similar livestock (sheep, cattle, and goats); worked similar metals (mostly bronze, until iron technology was developed); and grew many similar crops (including emmer wheat, barley, cucumbers, and onions). But climate and customs differed. Each culture had its own history and has left a unique legacy for us to treasure.

Acknowledgments

Many people helped with this book. I owe them my gratitude.

My first thanks go to the experts who graciously reviewed the manuscript for accuracy. Scott Noegel, Ph.D., Assistant Professor at the University of Washington's Department of Near East Languages and Civilization, reviewed the earliest stage of the manuscript and encouraged and guided me, responding to my numerous questions, until its final form. Gary Beckman, Ph.D., professor of Hittite and Mesopotamian Studies at the University of Michigan and Associate Editor, *Journal of the American Oriental Society*, generously reviewed the manuscript in detail more than once and contributed the Hittite cuneiform when I despaired of transcribing it correctly. Bruce Williams, Ph.D., former Research Associate of the University of Chicago's Oriental Institute Museum, kindly reviewed an early version of the Nubia section. Emily Teeter, Ph.D., associate curator of the Oriental Institute Museum, graciously reviewed a later stage of the Nubia section and provided invaluable feedback on very short notice. Any errors that remain are my own.

My next thanks go to the children. I am especially grateful to the regular Wednesday-night craft-testers: Alisen Downey, Amara Rodriguez, Kristine Smith, and Omri and Erez Younker. Thanks also to other children for their help: Ben Coleman, Colin Cook, Katie Dupar, Lily Sol Harris, Ian Herrick, Morgan Houghton, Naomi Kreeger, Maddie Levy, Jason Quesnell, Ally and Kiley Reardon, Naomi Rubin, Gus Seixas, Emily Spence, Alissa Stempson, Clark Sutherland, Robin Trainor, Keegan Uchacz, and Kristen Usher. I send thanks also to Stephanie Cannon for facilitating my work with not one but two elementary schools. From Montlake Elementary, classes of 1998–99, I thank Joan McBride and Lauren Bernard and their

K–1 students; Karen Jones and her fourth- and fifth-grade students Gerard, Gracie, Hailey, and Anders; and especially Gail Schalk and her fourth- and fifth-grade class for their enthusiastic testing of activities. At Woodmoor Elementary, I thank Steve Vanderhijde and five of his sixth grade students: Heather Jacobsen, Jaime Patneaude, Danielle Peyton, Sara Sullivan, and Megan Wellnitz; also from Woodmoor, students Sarah Michelle Dumford, Katie Fink, Evangelynn Honegger-Kizanis, Tiffany Stusinski, and Erin Thompson. Thanks also go to Mrs. Crighton and her 1995–96 fifth-grade class at Arbor Heights Elementary.

I'm grateful to the adults who read the manuscript or refined activities: Laurie Almoslino, Ellen Baker, Lynn Chapman, Amy Davis, Miriam Driss, Frannie and Ron Ein, Gail Gensler, Susan Locke, Gloria London, Priscilla Long, Dean Napolitan, Stephanie Rubin, Tracy Salter, Lona Sepessey, Gary Schajer, Fayla Schwartz, Beverly Slatin, and Reed and Barbara Sutherland.

For help with the art, I thank Carlton T. Hodge, Professor Emeritus of Linguistics at Indiana University; Sara Campbell, Bonnie Wachtel, and Sylvia Broida. For translation help, I thank Önol Bilkur and Helena Valkova.

For assistance with research, I thank Monica Blanchard of Catholic University; Carole Krucoff of the Oriental Institute; and the reference staff at the northeast and downtown branches of Seattle Public Library. Thanks go, also, to Altay Yalcin, Ali Turkcan, and Gül Civelekoglu; Begümsen Ergenekon of the Middle East Technical University in Ankara; and Yasemin Arikan, Gül Ün, Esma Reyhan, and Leyla Murat of A.Ü. D.T.C.

I am grateful to Eisenbrauns, publishers, for permission to adapt the recipe for sebetu rolls from page 11 of their 1995 book, *Textes Culinaires Mésopotomiens: Mesopotamian Culinary Texts* by Jean Bottéro. I am also grateful to the Egypt Exploration Society for permission to adapt the Meroitic tomb inscription from F. Ll. Griffith's 1912 book, page 57, *Meroitic Inscriptions, Part II, Napata to Philas and Miscellaneous.*

I also thank Suzy Harris and Tom Coleman; Marie Moffitt; Elsa Richmond; Maureen Jackson; Erica Schrack; Christopher Kerr; Pat Richmond, Steve LaSala, and Ann Davidge. Special thanks go to Cynthia Sherry and my editor, Lisa Rosenthal, of Chicago Review Press, and to my agent, Marian Reiner, without whom this book would not exist. And finally to those whose names I inadvertently omitted, you have my appreciation!

Children's Books for Further Reading

Bartók, Mira. *Ancient Egypt and Nubia*. Glenview, IL: Good Year Books, 1995.

Bianchi, Steven. *The Nubians: People of the Ancient Nile*. Brookfield, CT: The Millbrook Press, 1994.

Bunting, Eve. *I Am the Mummy Heb-Nefert*. New York: Harcourt Brace & Co., 1997.

Corbishley, Mike. *The Ancient World*. New York: Peter Bedrick Books, 1992.

Crosher, Judith. *Ancient Egypt*. New York: Viking, 1992.

Hart, Avery and Paul Mantell. *Pyramids! 50 Hands-on Activities to Experience Ancient Egypt*. Charlotte, VT: Williamson Publishing, 1997.

Hart, George. *Ancient Egypt*. New York: Knopf, 1990.

Jenkins, Earnestine. *A Glorious Past: Ancient Egypt, Ethiopia, and Nubia*. New York: Chelsea House Publishers, 1995.

Millard, Anne. *How People Lived*. New York: Dorling Kindersley, Inc. 1989.

Odjik, Pamela. *The Sumerians*. The Ancient World Series. Englewood Cliffs, NJ: Silver Burdett Press, 1990.

Unstead, R.J., ed. *See Inside an Egyptian Town*. New York: Warwick Press, 1986.

Bibliography

Egyptians

Andreu, Guillemette. *Egypt in the Age of the Pyramids*, translated by David Lorton. Ithaca, NY: Cornell University Press, 1997.

Baines, John and Jaromir Malek. *Atlas of Ancient Egypt*. New York: Facts on File, 1980.

Darby, William J.; Paul Ghalioungui; and Louis Grivetti. *Food: The Gift of Osiris, Volumes 1 and 2*. New York: Academic Press, 1977.

David, A. R., ed., *Mysteries of the Mummies*. London: Cassell, 1978.

Davies, W. V. *Egyptian Hieroglyphics*. Berkeley: University of California Press, 1987.

Edwards, I. E. S. *The Pyramids of Egypt, New Edition*. New York: Viking, 1985.

Haab, Sherri and Laura Torres. *The Incredible Clay Book*. Palo Alto, CA: Klutz, 1994.

Hart, George. *Eyewitness Books: Ancient Egypt*. New York: Alfred A. Knopf, 1990.

Hobson, Christine. *The World of the Pharaohs: A Complete Guide to Ancient Egypt*. London: Thames and Hudson, 1987.

Hollis, Susan Tower. "Tales of Magic and Wonder from Ancient Egypt." In Jack Sasson et al., eds., *Civilizations of the Ancient Near East*. New York: Charles Scribner's Sons, 1995, pp. 2255–2264.

Janssen, Rosalind. "Costume in New Kingdom Egypt." In Jack Sasson et al., eds., *Civilizations of the Ancient Near East*. New York: Charles Scribner's Sons, 1995, pp. 383–394.

Kemp, Barry J. "Unification and Urbanization of Ancient Egypt." In Jack Sasson et al., eds., *Civilizations of the Ancient Near East*. New York: Charles Scribner's Sons, 1995, pp. 679–690.

Lesko, Leonard. "Death and the Afterlife in Ancient Egyptian Thought." In Jack Sasson et al., eds., *Civilizations of the Ancient Near East*. New York: Charles Scribner's Sons, 1995, pp. 1763–1774.

Lichtheim, Miriam. *Ancient Egyptian Literature, Volume I*. Berkeley, CA: University of California Press, 1975.

Murnane, William J. "The History of Ancient Egypt: An Overview." In Jack Sasson et al., eds., *Civilizations of the Ancient Near East*. New York: Charles Scribner's Sons, 1995, pp. 691–717.

Pinch, Geraldine. "Private Life in Ancient Egypt." In Jack Sasson et al., eds., *Civilizations of the Ancient Near East*. New York: Charles Scribner's Sons, 1995, pp. 363–382.

Putnam, James. *Eyewitness Books: Mummy*. New York: Alfred A. Knopf, 1992.

Renfrew, Jane. "Vegetables in the Ancient Near Eastern Diet." In Jack Sasson et al., eds., *Civilizations of the Ancient Near East*. New York: Charles Scribner's Sons, 1995, pp. 191–202.

Roberts, David. "Age of Pyramids: Egypt's Old Kingdom." *National Geographic*, January 1995, pp. 2–43.

Romano, James F. 1995. "Jewelry and Personal Arts in Ancient Egypt." In Jack Sasson et al., eds., *Civilizations of the Ancient Near East*. New York: Charles Scribner's Sons, 1995, pp. 1605–1613.

Sameh, Waley-el-dine. *Daily Life in Ancient Egypt*. Translated by Michael Bullock. New York: McGraw-Hill Book Co., 1964.

Samuel, Delwyn. "A New Look at Bread and Beer." *Egyptian Archaeology* 4, 1994, pp. 9–11.

Samuel, Delwyn. "Investigation of Ancient Egyptian Baking and Brewing Methods by Correlative Microscopy." *Science* 273, 1996, pp. 488–490.

Sewell, Barbara. *Egypt Under the Pharaohs*. New York: G. P. Putnam's Sons, 1968.

Time-Life Books. *Egypt: Land of the Pharaohs*. Alexandria, VA: Time-Life Books, 1992.

Tyldesley, Joyce. *Daughters of Isis: Women of Ancient Egypt*. New York: Viking, 1994.

Watson, Philip J. *Costume of Ancient Egypt*. New York: Chelsea House Publishers, 1987.

Wilson, John. *The Culture of Ancient Egypt*. Chicago: University of Chicago Press, 1951.

Winlock, H. E. *Models of Daily Life in Ancient Egypt*. Cambridge, MA: Harvard University Press, 1955.

Wu, C. "Ancient Bread Rises in Gourmet Status." *Science News* 150, 1996, p. 55.

Mesopotamians

Bahrani, Zainab. "Jewelry and Personal Arts in Ancient Western Asia." In Jack Sasson et al., eds., *Civilizations of the Ancient Near East*. New York: Charles Scribner's Sons, 1995, pp. 1635–1645.

Bier, Carol. "Textile Arts in Ancient Western Asia." In Jack Sasson et al., eds., *Civilizations of the Ancient Near East*. New York: Charles Scribner's Sons, 1995, pp. 1567–1588

Bottéro, Jean. "The Cuisine of Ancient Mesopotamia." *Biblical Archaeologist*, March 1985, pp. 36–47.

Bottéro, Jean. *Textes culinaires Mésopotamiens: Mesopotamian Culinary Texts*. Winona Lake, IN: Eisenbrauns, 1995.

Bottéro, Jean. *Writing, Reasoning and the Gods*, translated by Zainab Bahrani and Marc Van De Mieroop. Chicago: University of Chicago Press, 1992.

Collon, Dominique. "Clothing and Grooming in Ancient Western Asia." In Jack Sasson et al., eds., *Civilizations of the Ancient Near East*. New York: Charles Scribner's Sons, 1995, pp. 503–515.

Contenau, Georges. *Everyday Life in Babylon and Assyria.* Translated. New York: W. W. Norton & Company, Inc., 1966.

Editors of Time-Life Books. *Mesopotamia: the Mighty Kings*. Alexandria, VA: Time-Life Books, 1995.

Editors of Time-Life Books. *Sumer: Cities of Eden*. Alexandria, VA: Time-Life Books, 1993.

Farber, Walter. "Witchcraft, Magic, and Divination in Ancient Mesopotamia." In Jack Sasson et al., eds., *Civilizations of the Ancient Near East*. New York: Charles Scribner's Sons, 1995, pp.1899–1909.

Hesse, Brian. "Animal Husbandry and Human Diet in the Ancient Near East." In Jack Sasson et al., eds., *Civilizations of the Ancient Near East*. New York: Charles Scribner's Sons, 1995, pp 203–222.

Houston, Mary G. *Ancient Egyptian, Mesopotamian & Persian Costume and Decoration*. London: Adam & Charles Black, 2nd ed., 1954.

Kramer, Samuel Noah. *Cradle of Civilization*. Alexandria, VA: Time-Life Books, 1978.

Læssøe, Jørgen. *People of Ancient Assyria: Their Inscriptions and Correspondence*. Translated by F. S. Leigh-Browne. London: Routledge and Kegan Paul, 1963, pp. 103–106.

Mallowan, M. E. L. *Nimrud & Its Remains*. London: Collins, 1966.

Miglus, P. A., *Die Räumliche Organisation des Altbabylonischen Hofhauses* in Veenhof, Klaas R., (ed.), *Houses and Households in Ancient Mesopotamia*. Leiden, Netherlands: Nederlands Instituut voor het Nabije Oosten, 1996.

Moorey, P. R. S. *Ancient Mesopotamian Materials and Industries: The Archaeological Evidence*. Oxford: Clarendon Press, 1994.

Nemet-Nejat, Karen Rhea. *Daily Life in Ancient Mesopotamia*. Westport, CT: Greenwood Press, 1998.

Oppenheim, A. Leo. *Ancient Mesopotamia: Portrait of a Dead Civilization*, revised edition. Chicago: University of Chicago Press, 1977.

Pittman, Holly. "Cylinder Seals and Scarabs in the Ancient Near East." In Jack Sasson et al., eds., *Civilizations of the Ancient Near East*. New York: Charles Scribner's Sons, 1995, pp.1589–1603.

Postgate, J. N. *Early Mesopotamia: Society and Economy at the Dawn of History*. New York: Routledge, 1992.

Powell, Marvin A. "Metrology and Mathematics in Ancient Mesopotamia." In Jack Sasson et al., eds., *Civilizations of the Ancient Near East*. New York: Charles Scribner's Sons, 1995, pp. 1943–1954.

Renfrew, Jane M. "Vegetables in the Ancient Near Eastern Diet." In Jack Sasson et al., eds., *Civilizations of the Ancient Near East*. New York: Charles Scribner's Sons, 1995, pp. 191–202.

Roaf, Michael. *Cultural Atlas of Mesopotamia and the Ancient Near East*. New York: Facts on File, 1990.

Roaf, Michael. "Palaces and Temples in Ancient Mesopotamia." In Jack Sasson et al., eds., *Civilizations of the Ancient Near East*. New York: Charles Scribner's Sons, 1995, pp. 423–441.

Roth, Martha T. *Law Collections from Mesopotamia and Asia Minor*. 2nd edition. Atlanta: Scholars Press, 1997.

Saggs, H. W. F. *Peoples of the Past: Babylonians*. London: British Museum Press, 1995.

Scarre, Chris. *Smithsonian Timelines of the Ancient World: A Visual Chronology from the Origins of Life to AD 1500*. New York: Dorling Kindersley, 1993.

Schmandt-Besserat, Denise. "Record Keeping Before Writing." In Jack Sasson et al., eds., *Civilizations of the Ancient Near East*. New York: Charles Scribner's Sons, 1995, pp. 2097–2106.

Shaw, Ian. *Timeline of the Ancient World: 3000 B.C.-A.D. 500*. London: Bridgewater Press, 1994.

Van de Mieroop, Marc. *The Ancient Mesopotamian City*, Oxford: Clarendon Press, 1997.

Walker, C. B. F. *Reading the Past: Cuneiform*. Los Angeles: University of California Press, 1987.

Wiggermann, F. A. M., "Theologies, Priests, and Worship in Ancient Mesopotamia." In Jack Sasson et al., eds., *Civilizations of the Ancient Near East*. New York: Charles Scribner's Sons, 1995, pp. 1857–1870.

Woolley, Sir Leonard. *Ur Excavations, Volume V: The Ziggurat and Its Surroundings*. Oxford: University Press, 1939.

Nubians

Adams, William Y. "The Kingdom and Civilization of Kush in Northeast Africa." In Jack Sasson et al., eds., *Civilizations of the Ancient Near East*. New York: Charles Scribner's Sons, 1995, pp. 775–789.

Adams, William Y. *Nubia, Corridor to Africa*. Princeton: Princeton University Press, 1977.

Bradbury, L., "Following Tuthmosis I on his Campaign to Kush." *KMT: A Modern Journal of Ancient Egypt 3*, 1992, pp. 51–159, 76–77.

Butzer, Karl W. *Early Hydraulic Civilization in Egypt: A Study in Cultural Ecology*. Chicago: University of Chicago Press, 1976.

Davies, W. V., ed. *Egypt and Africa: Nubia from Prehistory to Islam*. London: British Museum Publications, 1991.

Dunham, Dows. *El Kurru*. Cambridge: Harvard University Press, 1950.

Emery, Walter B. *Lost Land Emerging*. New York: Charles Scribner's Sons, 1967.

Griffth, F. Ll., *Meroitic Inscriptions Part II: Napata to Philae and Miscellaneous*. London: William Clowes & Sons, Ltd., 1912.

Hintze, Fritz, and Ursula Hintze. *Civilizations of the Old Sudan*. Amsterdam: B. R. Grüner, 1968.

Kendall, Timothy. *Kerma and the Kingdom of Kush, 2500–1500 B.C.* Washington, DC: National Museum of African Art, Smithsonian Institution, 1997.

Kendall, Timothy. *Kush: Lost Kingdom of the Nile*. Brockton, MA: Brockton Art Museum/Fuller Memorial, 1982.

Kennedy, John G. *Nubian Ceremonial Life*. New York: The University of California Press, 1978.

O'Connor, David. *Ancient Nubia: Egypt's Rival in Africa*. Philadelphia: The University Museum, University of Pennsylvania, 1993.

Olson, Stacie and Josef Wegner. *Educational Guide: Ancient Nubia: Egypt's Rival in Africa*. Philadelphia: The University Museum, University of Pennsylvania, 1992.

Säve-Söderbergh, Torgny. *Temples & Tombs of Ancient Nubia: The International Rescue Campaign at Abu Simbel, Philae and Other Sites*, London: Thames and Hudson & Unesco, 1987.

Shinnie, P. L. *Ancient Nubia*, London: Kegan Paul International Ltd., 1996.

Shinnie, P. L. *Meroe: A Civilization of the Sudan*. New York: Frederick A. Praeger, 1967.

Svitil, Kathy A. "What the Nubians Ate: Mummies in Nubian Desert Reveal Clues to their Diet." *Discover 15*, June 1994, pp. 36–7.

Taylor, John H. *Egypt and Nubia*. Cambridge: Harvard Univeristy Press, 1991.

Thurman, Christa C. Mayer, and Bruce B. Williams. *Ancient Textiles from Nubia: Meroitic, X-Group and Christian Fabrics from Ballana and Qustul*. Chicago: The Art Institute of Chicago and the University of Chicago, 1979.

Trigger, Bruce G. *History and Settlement in Lower Nubia*. Yale University Publications in Anthropology 69. New Haven: Yale University, 1965.

Trigger, Bruce G. *Nubia under the Pharaohs*. London: Thames and Hudson, 1976.

Welsby, Derek A. *The Kingdom of Kush: the Napatan and Meroitic Empires*. London: British Museum Press, 1996.

Wenig, Steffen, ed. *Africa in Antiquity: The Arts of Ancient Nubia and the Sudan. Volumes I and II*. Brooklyn: The Brooklyn Museum, 1978.

Wildung, Dietrich, ed. *Sudan: Ancient Kingdoms of the Nile*. New York: Flammarion, 1997.

Williams, Bruce B. *Excavations Between Abu Simbel and the Sudan Frontier, Part 5: C-Group, Pan Grave, and Kerma Remains at Adindan Cemeteries T, K, U, and J*. Chicago: The Oriental Institute of the University of Chicago, 1983.

Williams, Bruce B. *Excavations Between Abu Simbel and the Sudan Frontier, Part 7: Twenty-fifth Dynasty and Napatan Remains at Qustul: Cemeteries W and V*. Chicago: The Oriental Institute of the University of Chicago, 1990.

Hittites

Beal, Richard H. "Hittite Military Organization." In Jack Sasson et al., eds., *Civilizations of the Ancient Near East*. New York: Charles Scribner's Sons, 1995, pp. 545–554.

Beckman, Gary. *Hittite Diplomatic Texts*. Atlanta: Scholars Press, 1996.

Beckman, Gary. "Royal Ideology and State Administration in Hittite Anatolia." In Jack Sasson et al., eds., *Civilizations of the Ancient Near East*. New York: Charles Scribner's Sons, 1995, pp. 529–543.

Bittel, Kurt. *Hattusha: The Capital of the Hittites*. New York: Oxford University Press, 1970.

Bryce, Trevor. *The Kingdom of the Hittites*. Oxford: Clarendon Press, 1998.

Canby, Jeanny Vorys. "The Child in Hittite Iconography." In Jeanny Vorys Canby et al., eds., *Ancient

Anatolia: Aspects of Change and Cultural Development. Madison, WI: The University of Wisconsin Press, 1986.

Doblhofer, Ernst. *Voices in Stone: The Decipherment of Ancient Scripts and Writings*. Translated by Mervyn Savill. London: Souvenir Press, Ltd, 1961.

Frantz-Szabó. "Hittite Witchcraft, Magic, and Divination." In Jack Sasson et al., eds., *Civilizations of the Ancient Near East*. New York: Charles Scribner's Sons, 1995, pp. 2007–2019.

Friedrich, Johannes. *Extinct Languages*. Translated by Frank Gaynor. New York: Dorset Press, 1957.

Gurney, O. R. *Some Aspects of Hittite Religion*. Oxford: Oxford University Press, 1977.

Gurney, O. R. *The Hittites*. New York: Viking Penguin, 1990.

Güterbock, Hans G. "Resurrecting the Hittites." In Jack Sasson et al., eds., *Civilizations of the Ancient Near East*. New York: Charles Scribner's Sons, 1995, pp. 2765–2777.

Hoffner, Harry A., Jr. *Alimenta Hethaeorum: Food Production in Hittite Asia Minor*. New Haven: American Oriental Society, 1974.

Hoffner, Harry A. Jr. "Legal and Social Institutions of Hittite Anatolia." In Jack Sasson et al., eds., *Civilizations of the Ancient Near East*. New York: Charles Scribner's Sons, 1995, pp 555–569.

Houwink ten Cate, H. J. Philo, and Folke Josephson. "Muwatallis' Prayer to the Storm-God of Kummami." *Revue Hittite et Asianique, XXV*, 81, 1967, pp. 102–150.

Imparati, Fiorella. "Private Life Among the Hittites." In Jack Sasson et al., eds., *Civilizations of the Ancient Near East*. New York: Charles Scribner's Sons, 1995, pp. 571–586.

Laroche, Lucienne. *Monuments of Civilization: The Middle East*. New York: Grosset & Dunlap, 1974.

Lloyd, Seton. *Ancient Turkey: A Traveller's History of Anatolia*. Berkeley: University of California Press, 1989.

MacQueen, J. G. *The Hittites and Their Contemporaries in Asia Minor*, revised edition. London: Thames and Hudson, 1986.

Sturtevant, Edgar H. and Adelaide E. Hahn. *A Comparative Grammar of the Hittite Language*. New Haven: Yale University Press, 1951.

Sturtevant, Edgar H. and George Bechtel. *A Hittite Chrestomathy*. Philadelphia: University of Pennsylvania, 1935.

Sturtevant, Edgar H. *A Hittite Glossary*. 2nd ed. Philadelphia: University of Pennsylvania, 1936.

Trade

Astour, Michael C. "Overland Trade Routes in Ancient Western Asia." In Jack Sasson et al., eds., *Civilizations of the Ancient Near East*. New York: Charles Scribner's Sons, 1995, pp. 1401–1420.

Veenhof, Klaas R. "Kanesh: An Assyrian Colony in Anatolia." In Jack Sasson et al., eds., *Civilizations of the Ancient Near East*. New York: Charles Scribner's Sons, 1995, pp. 859–871.

Index